10-

P9-CEX-873

OTHER PUBLICATIONS:
MYSTERIES OF THE UNKNOWN
TIME FRAME
FIX IT YOURSELF
FITNESS, HEALTH & NUTRITION
SUCCESSFUL PARENTING
HEALTHY HOME COOKING
UNDERSTANDING COMPUTERS
LIBRARY OF NATIONS
THE ENCHANTED WORLD
THE KODAK LIBRARY OF CREATIVE PHOTOGRAPHY
GREAT MEALS IN MINUTES
THE CIVIL WAR
PLANET EARTH
COLLECTOR'S LIBRARY OF THE CIVIL WAR
THE EPIC OF FLIGHT
THE GOOD COOK
WORLD WAR II
HOME REPAIR AND IMPROVEMENT
THE OLD WEST

For information on and a full description of any of the
Time-Life Books series listed above, please write:

Reader Information
Time-Life Customer Service
P.O. Box C-32068
Richmond, Virginia 23261-2068

This Fabulous Century

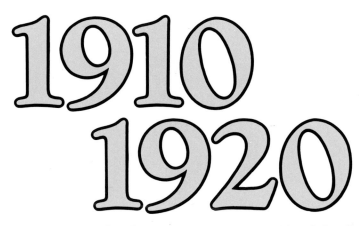

1910
1920

By the Editors of TIME-LIFE BOOKS

Time-Life Books, Alexandria, Virginia

THIS FABULOUS CENTURY

Contents

America 1910-1920

Omaha wedding party, about 1912.

Midwestern park, 1911.

Immigrant laborers, about 1911.

Brooklyn pier, 1914.

Soft-drink promoter, Vermont, about 1910.

Nebraska prairie, 1916.

New York sweet-potato vendor, about 1912.

America's largest flag, made in Manchester, New Hampshire, 1914.

Front-page stories record the anguish of a decade, from Mark Twain's epoch-ending death, through a great war abroad, to increasing violence and disillusion at home.

The End of Innocence

America is in a period of clamor, of bewilderment, of an almost tremulous unrest. We are hastily reviewing all our social conceptions. We are profoundly disenchanted.

THE NEW DEMOCRACY BY WALTER WEYL, 1912

"Whither Are We Drifting?" Such was the title of a worried sermon delivered by the Reverend James K. Thompson in Muskogee, Oklahoma, on June 28, 1914. It was an old theme, shopworn by generations of preachers, but the question never had seemed more pertinent to life in the United States. For the second decade of the century was a perplexing time for Americans.

On the positive side, they saw the continuance of the economic growth of the previous decade. The gross national product rose from $30.4 billion in 1910 to $71.6 billion in 1920. More and more people, benefiting from mass production, shared in the "good life"; Americans bought some 10 million passenger cars during those 10 years. The statistics, or at least many of the statistics, bore out the glowing assurances of a 1917 article in *Hearst's* magazine: "Never before was capital so plentiful. Never before were such profits rolled up by corporations. Never before were such wages enjoyed."

Yet these affluent times were roiled by increasing ferment and discontent. Labor unrest, rising little noticed in the previous decade, could no longer be ignored; in the first six months of 1916, the country was beset by no fewer than 2,093 strikes and lockouts. Added to the demands of militant labor were strident voices campaigning for other causes that seemed even more radical than the six-day work week: woman suffrage, birth control, advancement for colored people, progressive education, prohibition. Most alarming of all, a million socialists were demanding the overthrow of capitalism, which—they asserted—had proved itself rotten to the core.

Where, indeed, were we drifting?

Actually, the United States was no more adrift than it had ever been. Rather, it had entered a new period of hectic change. A host of problems, most of them arising from headlong industrialization, faced the country as it struggled to catch up with modern times. New necessities clashed violently with old traditions, inflaming antagonisms of every sort. By 1920 the crises of the times had taken many casualties, among them America's easy optimism and naive self-assurance.

The new doubts of this stormy period, rooted in the conflicting strengths and weaknesses of American society, were summed up in the person of the man who was President during most of the decade: Woodrow Wilson. In contrast to Theodore Roosevelt, who typified the unquestioning confidence of the first decade, Wilson was introspective, querulous and complex; he could say ruefully, "I am a vague, conjectural personality, more made up of opinions and academic prepossessions than of human traits and red corpuscles." He was a minority President, winning election by only 41.9 per cent of the popular vote in 1912 and by 49.3 per cent in 1916. And yet Wilson represented the great majority in his attitudes toward the two major dilemmas of the decade: social reform at home and relations with foreign nations.

When Wilson asked Congress to declare war on Germany, America reached the point of no return in its accelerating shift away from isolation toward international involvement. The President and his countrymen knew this and they agonized over the decision. But when they finally chose involvement, they did so on a basis that revealed America's lack of international experience. Wilson's war message urged the nation to launch a selfless crusade "for the right of those who submit to authority to have a voice in their own Governments, for the rights and liberties of small nations, for a universal dominion of right." The country ardently embraced these idealistic goals—and thus set a course for postwar disillusionment.

Even more ironic, the democratic principles that Americans were willing to die for in Europe were badly in need of defense at home. Free speech and the freedom of the press were curtailed in the name of patriotism, and anyone whose name, manner or ideas seemed unorthodox to self-styled "100 per cent Americans" was viciously harassed. This bigotry could not be explained away as a passing manifestation of wartime hysteria. Well before America entered the war, the pressures of national problems stirred hatemongers to attack ethnic and religious minorities. A classic case of anti-Semitism exploded in Georgia in 1913. Leo Frank, the well-to-do manager of an Atlanta pencil factory, was convicted of murder on highly questionable evidence. When the governor commuted the death sentence, a mob of irate Georgians abducted Frank from the state prison and lynched him.

Such denials of fundamental justice were bound up with the broader problem of protecting the rights of all American citizens. In this decade the problem focused most sharply on the plight of labor. One third to one half of the working population toiled up to 12 hours daily—sometimes seven days a week—for bare subsistence wages and lived in urban slums or factory-town shanties. This exploitation of human beings appalled Americans loyal to traditions of fair play, equal justice and equal opportunity. Their reaction was expressed by the senior sage of American letters, William Dean Howells: "When our country is wrong she is worse than other countries when they are wrong because she has more light than other countries, and we ought somehow to make her feel that we are sorry and ashamed for her."

Americans announced their shame in the democratic manner. Voting their conscience, they elected to office three successive Presidents—Roosevelt, Taft and Wilson—whose platforms promised to improve working conditions and to curb the powers of monopolies. To most Americans, including Wilson, this was about as far as government regulation should go.

But to the great masses of the poor in America's labor force, this brand of reform was too little and too late. The unions found it increasingly difficult to gain recognition or concessions from the managers of Big Business, who felt that their property rights were threatened by the workers' demands. The working man remained an outsider looking in on the "good life," and his patience was fast running out. Beyond simply suffering in silence he had little choice but to leave the job and seek a more generous employer, or to strike. Workers voted for more and more strikes, strikes of increasing desperation and anger, strikes met by violence from company guards, thuggish strikebreakers, and often the local police and the state militia. The usual attitude of the corporation managers was bluntly set forth by one hard-boiled executive: "If a workman sticks up his head, hit it!"

Many heads got hit—and worse. In 1914 during a seven-month strike by 9,000 Colorado coal miners, a small army of company guards attacked a workers' encampment and raked it with gunfire for hours, killing at least 21 men

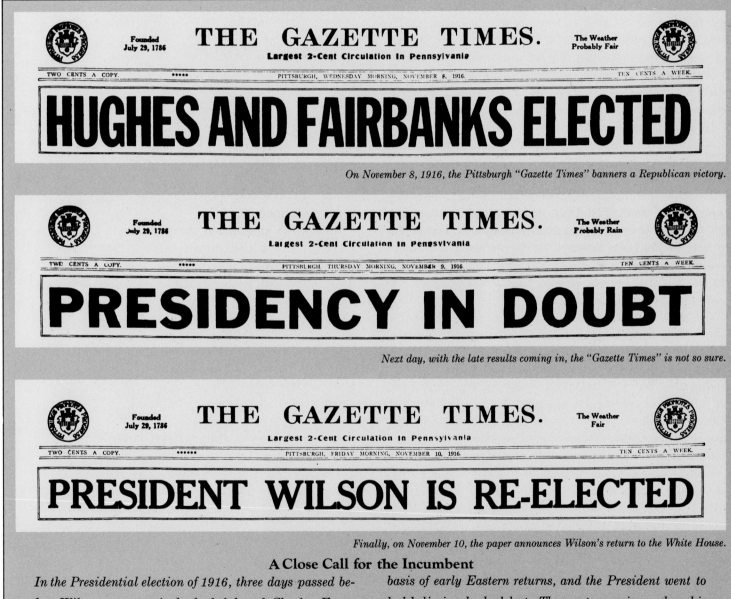

THE GAZETTE TIMES.

Founded July 29, 1786

Largest 2-Cent Circulation in Pennsylvania

The Weather Probably Fair

TWO CENTS A COPY.   PITTSBURGH, WEDNESDAY MORNING, NOVEMBER 8, 1916.   TEN CENTS A WEEK.

HUGHES AND FAIRBANKS ELECTED

On November 8, 1916, the Pittsburgh "Gazette Times" banners a Republican victory.

THE GAZETTE TIMES.

Founded July 29, 1786

Largest 2-Cent Circulation in Pennsylvania

The Weather Probably Rain

TWO CENTS A COPY.   PITTSBURGH, THURSDAY MORNING, NOVEMBER 9, 1916.   TEN CENTS A WEEK.

PRESIDENCY IN DOUBT

Next day, with the late results coming in, the "Gazette Times" is not so sure.

THE GAZETTE TIMES.

Founded July 29, 1786

Largest 2-Cent Circulation in Pennsylvania

The Weather Fair

TWO CENTS A COPY.   PITTSBURGH, FRIDAY MORNING, NOVEMBER 10, 1916.   TEN CENTS A WEEK.

PRESIDENT WILSON IS RE-ELECTED

Finally, on November 10, the paper announces Wilson's return to the White House.

A Close Call for the Incumbent

In the Presidential election of 1916, three days passed before Wilson was certain he had defeated Charles Evans Hughes by carrying California. But on election night, many newspapers, including the Pittsburgh "Gazette Times" (above), were claiming a Hughes victory on the basis of early Eastern returns, and the President went to bed believing he had lost. The next morning, when his daughter informed him that "The New York Times" had declared the election "unsettled," Wilson greeted the news skeptically. He retorted, "You tell that to the Marines!"

and wounding 100. Predictably, the roughest treatment was reserved for the most radical union, the socialistic Industrial Workers of the World. I.W.W. members, the so-called Wobblies, were mutilated and lynched in Butte, Montana, and Centralia, Washington. As war hysteria took hold in Bisbee, Arizona, in 1917, more than 1,100 striking Wobbly miners were routed out of bed by a vigilante band, herded at gunpoint into cattle cars and dumped in a New Mexican desert without food or water. They were later put in an Army stockade for two months—until the strike was broken—and their appeals to President Wilson for intercession were pointedly ignored.

In the aftermath of the war, Wilson himself reaped the whirlwind of frustrated idealism. At the Paris Peace Conference, his Fourteen Points for a "peace without victory" were whittled down to a disappointing nub; the Senate and the country, weary of war, tumult and change, rejected the League of Nations.

With the disavowal of Wilson came one of the ugliest periods in American history. Race riots broke out in many urban centers, and the revived Ku Klux Klan fomented hatred even in the relatively enlightened Northeast. Drumhead justice was the order of the day for dissenters and radicals of every stripe. On one night alone—January 2-3, 1920—some 5,000 alleged "Reds" were taken prisoner in simultaneous raids in scores of cities, and many aliens among them were deported without due process. Men of good will recoiled in horror and shame.

America was, as an English visitor said, "a nation sitting in judgment on itself." It had handed down a solemn verdict in favor of reform at home and involvement abroad, and these commitments were irreversible even though political reaction and renewed isolationism temporarily held sway. More and more Americans, their ingenuous self-confidence severely shaken, were willing to test new ideas, to discard outmoded values. More and more they came to accept the modern era on its own grim terms. They knew now that life would never again be simple. They realized that hard work, self-reliance and faith in God were no longer enough. America was growing up.

In 1915 "Harper's Weekly" ran this montage of newspaper articles to underscore America's extremes of wealth and poverty—a source of deep unrest during the decade.

Emancipated ladies try out men's pipes, drinks and haberdashery.

The New Woman

The Many Faces of a New Freedom

Her skirts have just reached her very trim and pretty ankles; her hair, coiled upon her skull, has just exposed the ravishing whiteness of her neck. A charming creature!
H. L. MENCKEN

Every year some new fashion comes to remind us that woman is still a savage.
DR. MAX BAFF, A MASSACHUSETTS SCIENTIST

The age-old battle between the sexes took a new and unsettling turn during the decade. A fresh ingredient was provided by the emergence of a new kind of female, one who smoked cigarettes, drove automobiles, bobbed her hair and generally kicked up her heels in a manner that shocked her conservative elders.

Declaring her independence and her equality with men, this emancipated lady discarded the pinched-in corsets and cumbersome petticoats worn by her older sister and went off to earn her own living. She demanded, and eventually she got, the right to vote and hold political office. According to *The Ladies' Home Journal*, she was "independent, bright-eyed, alert, alive."

Her new-found freedom sometimes took outlandish forms. A particularly emancipated crew of bohemian ladies, led by a Greenwich Village anarchist named Emma Goldman, advocated free love. Miss Goldman, attacking the double standard that prescribed chastity for women but not for men, gave lectures in which she challenged every man in the audience who had made no amorous conquests before marriage to declare himself. Few ever did.

The men of the decade reacted to the phenomenon of the new women with decidedly mixed feelings. Some, like H. L. Mencken, the forward-looking editor of the magazine *Smart Set*, were entranced. To his comments above, he added, "There is something trim and trig and confident about her. She is easy in her manners. There is music in her laugh. She is youth, she is hope, she is romance—she is wisdom!"

Other males were horrified. The proper place for women, they felt, still was at home rearing children, and any attempt to assume a less domestic role would bring chaos. "We are living today," proclaimed a Brooklyn priest, "in a pandemonium of powder, a riot of rouge, and moral anarchy of dress." Another commentator declared that women were not entirely human, but "a sub-species set apart for purposes of reproduction, merely."

Even some females looked askance at the new woman and suspected that she was somehow no longer quite feminine. The poetess Ella Wheeler Wilcox grumbled that "she has shown her pitiful lack of common sense, in the last score of years, by her persistent acquisition of masculine, old-world vices"—presumably meaning that she now smoked and drank sherry. And journalist Ida Tarbell, in an article in *The American Magazine*, posed the question of the decade: "Is woman making a man of herself?"

Society ladies were among the first to smoke; this proper young debutante, dressed for a swim, tries an awkward puff on the beach at Southampton, Long Island.

The new woman took control of things, whether she was sitting at the steering ropes of a bobsled team at Locust Valley, New York (top), or at the wheel of a snappy Ford.

Among the decade's female pioneers were one of the first women pilots, Blanche Scott, (top), and lady tipplers at the bar of New York City's Majestic Hotel.

"Heaven will protect the working girl," Broadway star Marie Dressler had sung in 1910, and within 10 years Heaven must have had its hands full. At the start of the second decade, some 7.5 million women were in gainful occupations; by 1920 this figure had jumped to more than 8.5 million and showed no signs of slackening. Suddenly the heretofore sacrosanct male business world seemed to be engulfed by a wave of skirted secretaries *(top left)*, sales people *(top right)* and telephone operators *(center, leaving work in Washington, D.C.)*. Though many men reacted with rage, others, like the anonymous British writer quoted at far right in a 1914 issue of the *New York American*, fairly glowed with pleasure at seeing women on the job.

About the average American woman of the middle-classes there can be no doubt at all. She is incomparably the smartest, most elegant and beautiful thing that exists under Heaven. It is not of the women of fashion I speak, though many are lovely enough. It is the ordinary, everyday-go-to-work girl who takes her lunch at Child's, runs to catch a trolley-car, jostles you in the subway, and patronizes what you call the cinematograph theatre and she calls the "movies." It is, in fact, the goddess of the typewriter, the fairy of the newspaper office, the grace of the telephone that I sing.

When the emancipated woman slid into the new styles of the decade, it was obvious to admiring males she was freeing herself of more than social restraints. Gone was the tight corset that had pinched in her waist until she could barely breath. Now, if her figure tended to spread out, then so be it. But by 1914 (right), haute couture had imposed some new strictures, and skirts had become so tight that walking was all but impossible.

1910

1914

"Never in history were the modes so abhorrently indecent as they are today," scolded one clergyman in 1913—needlessly. For while ladies' skirts were shorter, high-buttoned shoes often concealed ankles. And though skirts were sometimes transparent, they disclosed only patterned linings. Such beguiling sensuality did not last. After the war, the styles of 1920 (right) were about as sexy as the Salvation Army uniforms they tried to copy.

1917

1920

One more barrier between the sexes comes crashing down as a Milwaukee women's swimming team appears in a chic and revealing collection of men's swim suits.

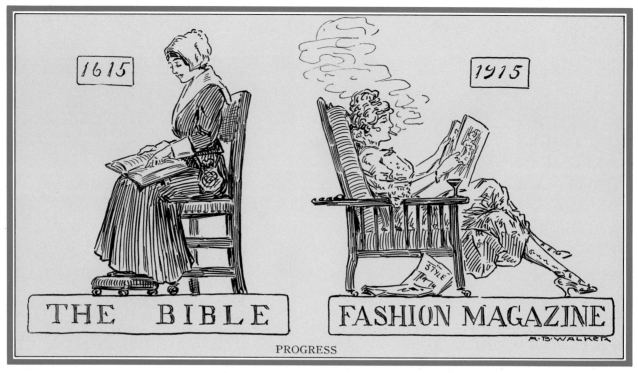

PROGRESS

"OF WHAT IS THIS WOMAN ACCUSED?" "FEMININITY, YOUR HONORESS." "SIX MONTHS!"

"SMOKING JACKETS? YES, MA'AM—FOR A LADY OR A GENTLEMAN, MA'AM?"

The emancipated woman, already denounced by both pulpit and press, was acidly lampooned by contemporary wits in cartoons from the humor magazine "Life."

The Big Breakthrough

On a rainy May afternoon in 1910, an unlikely army of hobble-skirted matrons and bright-eyed young girls trudged down New York City's Fifth Avenue to demand an American right denied only to criminals, lunatics, idiots and women—the right to vote. Many of the marchers, their spirits dampened by the chill drizzle and the jeers of skeptical bystanders, dropped out and the parade fizzled. Nevertheless, it was significant as the decade's opening volley in a long-fought battle for female suffrage.

Ever since the middle of the previous century, a small cadre of militants had been clamoring for the vote. Stern-faced ladies with deceptively old-fashioned names, such as Lucretia Coffin Mott, Elizabeth Cady Stanton and Susan B. Anthony, kept up a steady demand for women's rights. But by the end of the century they had won the right to vote in only four states.

In the emancipated mood of 1910, however, the suffrage movement gained national impetus. Women began holding rallies, giving speeches, lobbying in Congress and parading in ever greater numbers. Housewives and secretaries wore the traditional yellow color of the cause and sported corsages of yellow daisies, jonquils and buttercups. Mrs. O.H.P. Belmont, a *grande dame* of New York society, formed a Political Equality Association and ordered from England a specially designed tea service decorated with the slogan "Votes for Women." Actresses Lillian Russell and Mrs. Otis Skinner joined the movement. Suddenly, suffrage was fashionable.

The opposition, consisting of male holdouts and assorted females who felt voting was not quite nice, staged a last-ditch stand with counter-demonstrations and magazine articles. The humor magazine *Puck* impishly predicted "a long line of skimpy skirts tackling an election booth—each one having to stop and powder her nose, and fix her hair, and adjust her belt, and look through her handbag, and wonder who the occupant of the next booth is voting for; the elections would have to be held 'the first two weeks in November.' " But as the pros and antis continued to shout their feelings with climactic vehemence (*overleaf*), the pressures to give women the vote became irresistible.

In a grassroots campaign to win the right to vote, these ladies of the Equal Suffrage League of St. Louis, Missouri, visit one of the state's small country towns.

The New Woman

Mrs. O.H.P. Belmont speaks at a suffragist tea.

A curbside fund raiser, clutching a contribution basket, draws a bemused crowd.

I am sick to death of this shriek for women's rights. It is doing more harm than good among women. I wish all women felt as I do; I have more rights now than I can properly attend to.

MAY IRWIN, ACTRESS

We couldn't make a worse mess of it than the men, and we might do better.

AN ASPIRING WOMAN VOTER

I am suffering enough now and am really too busy to bother with the suffrage movement at all.

AN ANONYMOUS HOUSEWIFE

I believe in woman's suffrage wherever the women want it. Where they do not want it, the suffrage should not be forced upon them.

THEODORE ROOSEVELT

If anything is coming to us, we want it.

AN ANONYMOUS WOMAN

I would rather die and go to hell than vote for woman suffrage!

MEMBER OF THE MISSISSIPPI HOUSE OF REPRESENTATIVES

A suffragist band drums up interest for a concert in Hackensack, New Jersey.

A soapbox orator gives a feminist harangue.

The suffragists are bringing us to the culmination of a decadence which has been steadily indicated by race suicide, divorce, break-up of the home, and federalism, all of which conditions are found chiefly in primitive society.

ANTI-SUFFRAGETTE MAGAZINE, THE WOMAN PATRIOT

It is only the poltroon, the misguided fool, and the man with a Sixteenth-Century mind who opposes their entrance into the political arena.

THE NASHVILLE TENNESSEAN

Woman suffrage can make the Statue of Liberty look 10 miles taller to every despairing victim of Old-World conditions.

PHILADELPHIA PUBLIC LEDGER

By keeping women out of politics, the soul of our country is diminished by one-half.

NATIONAL WOMAN SUFFRAGE ASSOCIATION

I'm with you. I'm for it. I'll vote for it. Now don't bother me.

NEW YORK STATE REPRESENTATIVE FIORELLO LA GUARDIA

A staunch campaigner hands out pamphlets in a New York City barbershop.

Its ranks swelling daily through the enlistment of earnest ladies like the one at right, the suffrage movement staged a series of public rallies that grew ever larger, louder and more festive. In 1912 some 15,000 ladies high-stepped up Fifth Avenue, cheered by a crowd of half a million. This was outdone, three years later, by a procession of 40,000, including a large contingent from the Men's League for Woman Suffrage. In Seattle, where women were given the vote in 1910, the suffragists celebrated with a mass rally in the Opera House; the hall, festooned with crossed brooms and placards announcing "A Clean Sweep," was packed to capacity. In Washington, D.C., a march on the Capitol in 1914 took on the pomp of a military processional, with 10 bands, 50 ladies on horseback and platoons of government dignitaries. During such rallies, the anonymous women in the ranks felt a heady new sense of unity and purpose, as described below in *The Outlook* magazine by a suffragist marcher in the Fifth Avenue parade of 1915.

I *didn't walk in New York's first suffrage parade because my mother wouldn't let me. Next year, in 1913, I wanted to march, but my husband asked me not to. This fall I decided that it was "up to me" to suffer for democracy.*

Three o'clock on the afternoon of October 23, and a glorious day. Every band in Greater New York and some beyond blows like the breeze today. First it's "Tipperary," then "Tipperary" again, and once more "Tipperary."

After fifty false alarms, suddenly down the line comes the signal, "Make ready." Quickly we slip into place. The marshals look us over, straighten out bends and kinks, and then, as the band strikes up, begin to count time, "Left, left, left!" My heart is thumping louder than the band. Dear heaven, we're there!

By the time we had gone two blocks I had forgotten everything I had expected to feel. All my girlhood Mother had repeated that a lady should never allow herself to be conspicuous. To march up Fifth Avenue had promised to flout directly one's early training. I was mistaken. There's no notoriety about it. When it's done along with twenty-five thousand other women, nothing could seem more natural. Embarrassment is left at the street corner, and one is just a part, a singing, swinging part of a great stream, all flowing in the same direction toward the same goal.

It wasn't all smooth going. By five o'clock the wind had ris-en, and the banners became increasingly strenuous. Some burst their moorings and soared upwards with the breeze. The long garlands of laurel which bound us together, stretching from rank to rank, grew weightier with every block.

They tell us that two hundred and fifty thousand people watched us walk from Washington Square to Sixtieth Street. From sunlight till the moon came out, the chilly sidewalks never once were clear of the curious.

As we marched along I did not see the crowd. I never heeded the many policemen battling with the encroaching throng. Once, when we were marking time, an indignant woman burst through the sidelines and demanded of an overworked officer, "How can I get to the Grand Central Station in time to take my train?" "Well, ma'am," he drawled, "I don't see any better way than for you to fall into line and march there." "What, I in a suffrage parade!" she shrieked; "I wouldn't so demean myself," and flounced away. Another time I'd have thought that funny, but as we took up our procession I wondered what she meant. Thousands and thousands of women walking in protest before the bar of public opinion—could that be an unworthy thing? Could this, my new elation, multiplied twenty thousand fold, carry no impression to those who watched? Would even a Czar of autocratic Russia dare to disregard so great a demonstration of his people?

Warming up for a suffragist rally in Cambridge, Massachusetts, a young enthusiast mounts a soapbox in her back yard and takes a practice run through her speech.

On June 4, 1919, the women finally won. Congress passed the 19th Amendment to the Constitution, stating that no citizen could be denied the right to vote "on account of sex." The battle over, a shout of purest joy went up from the nation's 26 million newly enfranchised voters and their supporters. "The victory is not a victory for women alone," proclaimed the Kansas City *Star*, "it is a victory for democracy and the principle of equality upon which the nation was founded." A new era of clean government was prophesied. "The civilization of the world is saved," warbled James Cox, the Democratic candidate for President, in a bid for the votes of all 26 million saviors. But crusty old Joe Cannon, Speaker of the House, felt the changes might not be so great. He claimed, in an article from *The Delineator*, excerpted below, that women had in fact controlled the destiny of civilization for a long time.

It has been the privilege of women to advise, persuade and dictate ever since the first woman gave to the first man the fruit from the Tree of Knowledge and then shared with him the responsibility for that first disobedience, as well as the consciousness that fig-leaves were not in good form. She has led man into ways of wisdom and pleasantness or into ways of trouble throughout the history of the world.

I have had five generations of feminine influence in my own family to advise me, appeal to me and command me. My mother, reared in the Quaker faith where women were the equal of men, was my first counselor when I started out on the political road in 1860; then my wife took her place when I first came to Congress; then my daughters insisted on telling me what their father ought to do; later my granddaughters entered the family council, and now, in the first year of woman suffrage, my great-granddaughter in language not strictly parliamentary, but understood by her great-grandfather, gives advice and consent.

Celebrating their newly won right to vote, members of the National Woman's Party unfurl their star-studded banner at their headquarters in Washington, D.C.

The Flickers

Movie fans in New York City gather outside the picture show.

The High Art of Making Money

The motion picture is a great high art, not a process of commercial manufacture.

VACHEL LINDSAY

Films occupy fifth place among the industries of the United States, being surpassed by railroads, the clothing industry, iron and steel, and oil. The automobile-manufacturer is minor in importance.

THE PICTURE-PLAY MAGAZINE, 1916

Hollywood, California, in 1910 was a quiet country town near Los Angeles consisting of a few sprawling estates, dirt roads, lemon groves and a central square surrounded by churches. Its citizens included a large proportion of elderly people who had settled down to a placid retirement in the California sunshine. But in the first few years of the decade, Hollywood's tranquility was shattered by an influx of hustling newcomers who brought with them a bizarre enterprise they called the moving picture business. These invaders set up cameras on street corners, blocked traffic and cavorted about in strange costumes and make-up that frightened old ladies and small children. Local residents dubbed these obstreperous individuals "movies" and heartily wished they would go away.

They never did. By 1914 the word "movie" meant the product rather than the people, and there were 52 companies in and around Los Angeles spending $5,720,000 a year to churn out more than a thousand miles of developed film. Most of this production slid along on a noisome blend of high-handed profiteering and shady shenanigans that amounted at times to racketeering.

From the start, there had been something not quite respectable about the movies. The motion pictures cranked out around the turn of the century were anything but art. They consisted of flickering 10-minute sequences of faked newsreels, vaudeville skits, jittery travelogues and mildly pornographic episodes with titles like *What the Bootblack Saw* and *How Bridget Served the Salad Undressed.* The few professional actors who consented to appear in films usually did so secretly, concealing their shameful employment from their Broadway colleagues.

But while the gentility looked down their noses, the common folk lined up to pay the five-cent admission. New movie companies, centered in New York and Chicago, sprang up and prospered. And the unsavory aroma of their product was nothing compared to the outright stench from the industry itself. For the slash-belly competition among the producers had by 1910 erupted into full-scale war. It was fought in court battles, boycotts of movie houses and even violent skirmishes on the sets.

The basic trouble stemmed from a clever bit of legal jockeying on the part of Thomas A. Edison, who in 1889 had invented movies and who held patents on equipment and processes. In 1909 he pasted together a trust, the Motion Picture Patents Company, that enabled him to enforce a monopoly over movie production in America.

On location in the California hills, director Marshall Neilan (with glasses) poses super-star Mary Pickford in front of his cameras for a scene in "M'liss."

Fatty Arbuckle, Mabel Normand and the mutt typical of one-reel farces flounder in a Hollywood set during the filming of Mack Sennett's "Fatty and Mabel Adrift."

This left the nation's other movie makers with the option of joining Edison or quitting business. Most companies, such as Vitagraph, Selig, Essanay and Biograph, gave up and signed with the trust. But a few rough-playing mavericks, led by independent producers William Fox and Carl Laemmle, launched an aggressive attack on the trust in the courts of New York City, the nation's original movie capital.

The Patents Company retaliated with a series of low-hitting punches aimed somewhere about the knees. Trust studios pressured the independents' customers by cutting off shipments of films to movie houses that showed pictures made by the renegade companies. Cameras became impossible to buy and could be obtained only by theft or contraband shipment from Europe. A plague of mysterious accidents broke out in the independents' studios. Rolls of film caught fire or were destroyed by corrosive chemicals, cameras disappeared, and shooting sessions erupted into fist-swinging riots.

One by one, the independents began to look for havens from the trust. Most of them headed for Los Angeles, which offered not only good weather and steady sunshine for shooting—done almost entirely out of doors—but also a special bonus of extra-legal comfort: in case the police tried to confiscate bootleg cameras, the crew could run for Mexico, only 100 miles away.

Among the pioneer producers to make the cross-country trek from New York were Charles Bauman and Adam Kessel, two ex-bookies who had discovered that the odds for staying out of jail were probably better in making films than in betting horses. In 1909, after hired thugs had broken up one of their shooting sessions at Whitestone Landing on Long Island, sending five actors to the hospital, they started operations in a deserted grocery store outside Los Angeles. Others followed, commandeering rooftops, old buildings, vacant lots, any available space where they could set up their cameras.

The buccaneering tactics of the movie companies continued unabated in the California sunshine. Each studio operated in tight secrecy, behind high fences patrolled by armed guards. Sabotage and assault continued. When Cecil B. deMille arrived in Hollywood in 1913 to direct his first movie, *The Squaw Man*, he was shot at twice by snipers, the master copy of his film was destroyed by saboteurs, and he ended up carrying a loaded six-shooter.

Another, slightly more legal, method for knocking over a rival studio was to raid its talent, offering exorbitant salary increases to its best actors. The most earnestly raided players were the ingénues, dainty young girls with shy smiles and rippling curls. These coy damsels were the budding industry's No. 1 box-office attractions; but their names were carefully kept from the public by the movie trust in an attempt to keep their salaries down to a standard five dollars a day. Producers publicized the girls as anonymous properties of the studios, and audiences paid their nickels to see the Vitagraph Girl or the Biograph Girl. There was even, in 1911, a Vitagraph Dog.

But the cult of anonymity was broken by an independent producer, Carl Laemmle of Imp Studios, who cajoled the Biograph Girl away from her trust employers with promises of fame and more money. In an avalanche of newspaper publicity, he advertised his coup and disclosed the star's name as Florence Lawrence. Shortly thereafter, he staged another raid on Biograph and captured its "Little Mary" with a salary of $175 a week and crowed, "Little Mary is an Imp now." This new star, with her curls and dimples and the formal *nom de film* of Mary Pickford, quickly became the best-loved actress in the world.

Ultimately, sweet Little Mary turned out to be the cagiest maneuverer of them all. She deserted Laemmle and by an astute series of jumps from studio to studio parlayed her pay check to $10,000 a week by 1916. Others—including a growing number of freshly minted male stars—followed in her adroit footsteps and reaped similar benefits. As early as 1916, the authoritative fan magazine *Picture-Play* was moved to comment: "Salaries of players are, without a doubt, the greatest drain on the producers' bank-accounts. This can be readily realized when one brings to mind the single man who draws a salary that is nearly seven times that of the President of the United

States—Charlie Chaplin. Mr. Chaplin alone costs the Mutual Company $520,000 a year, and when his contract was signed he received an additional bonus of $150,000."

Though producers may have wept over the money they paid their stars, there was nothing but smiles for the money taken in at the box office. By 1916 some 25 million people a day spent anywhere from a nickel to a quarter to laugh at the antics of Mack Sennett's Keystone Kops or shiver at overacted, misplotted melodramas. Gross revenues from tickets had swelled to a whopping $735 million a year. The motion picture business had grown from a cutthroat squabble among fly-by-night operators into a major industry, the fifth largest in the nation. As *Picture-Play* noted, it was outstripped only by railroads, textiles, iron and steel, and oil; the automobile industry chugged along far behind, a poor sixth.

As the money poured in, leading producers, such as Cecil B. deMille, Lewis J. Selznick, Jesse Lasky and an ex-glove salesman born Sam Goldfish but better known as Samuel Goldwyn, began to budget ever increasing sums for individual pictures. Sets became more elaborate, film sequences were shot and edited with greater care, and the movies themselves became longer. The one-reel shorts of 1910, which had cost about $500 and taken only a few days to make, were giving way to two-hour features, costing $20,000, and finally to David Wark Griffith's super-colossal production, *Intolerance*, which cost a cool two million dollars and took two years to make *(page 73)*.

At the same time, other entrepreneurs were building lavish showcase movie theaters, such as the Regent and Rialto in New York City, resplendent with gilded columns, plush seats, uniformed ushers and 25-piece symphony orchestras. With these changes the "flickers" became not only respectable but even fashionable. When theater manager S. L. "Roxy" Rothafel opened the first of his famous Broadway motion picture houses, the Strand, in 1914, a critic from *The New York Times* wrote: "Going to the new Strand Theatre last night was very much like going to a Presidential reception, a first night at the opera or the opening of the horse show. It seemed like everyone in town had simultaneously arrived at the conclusion that a visit to the magnificent new movie playhouse was necessary."

Broadway too began to take a second look as top stage actors, suddenly aware that movies were no longer a "cheap show for cheap people," began hammering at the doors of Hollywood studios. The divine Sarah Bernhardt had already appeared in French films, declaring that "this is my one chance for immortality." Soon Minnie Maddern Fiske, Mrs. Leslie Carter, Billie Burke, and Weber and Fields left Broadway for excursions to the silent screen. "The insatiable maw of the silent drama," wrote the *Los Angeles Sunday Times* in 1914, "is daily, nay hourly, swallowing up the stars of other fields."

Before the end of the decade, motion pictures even earned a modest reputation as an art form. Serious critics were comparing Charlie Chaplin with Hamlet and a few giddy commentators went so far as to liken Mary Pickford to a Botticelli painting. The poet Vachel Lindsay claimed Thomas Edison was a "new Gutenberg" and wrote, "the invention of the photoplay is as great a step as was the beginning of picture-writing in the stone age."

Glowing in the new light of prosperity and respectability, the former border runners who headed the enormous new film industry gained an air of cocksure self-importance. After the overthrow of Czar Nicholas II in the revolution of 1917, Lewis J. Selznick, a Jewish immigrant who made good in the flickers, sent the cable below.

NICHOLAS ROMANOFF   *PETROGRAD, RUSSIA*

WHEN I WAS POOR BOY IN KIEV SOME OF YOUR POLICEMEN WERE NOT

KIND TO ME AND MY PEOPLE STOP I CAME TO AMERICA AND PROSPERED

STOP NOW HEAR WITH REGRET YOU ARE OUT OF A JOB OVER THERE STOP

FEEL NO ILLWILL WHAT YOUR POLICEMEN DID SO IF YOU WILL COME TO

NEW YORK CAN GIVE YOU FINE POSITION ACTING IN PICTURES STOP

SALARY NO OBJECT STOP REPLY MY EXPENSE STOP REGARDS YOU

AND FAMILY   *SELZNICK*

Three actors rehearsing a scene in the Jesse Lasky Feature Play Company huddle together to stay inside the white tapes indicating the camera's field of view.

THE ETHEREAL SISTERS

The Movie Queens: Saccharin, Strychnine and Sweet Sixteen

LILLIAN AND DOROTHY GISH, two sisters who exuded a rarefied aura of crushed lavender and moonbeams *(opposite),* were among the first representatives of a new phenomenon in America—the movie queen. They belonged to a celebrated handful of film actresses, some demure ingénues, some *femmes fatales,* who had come to symbolize through their movie roles the romantic ideals of the nation. An adoring public showered them with fan letters, and girls all over America tried to emulate their clothes, their hair styles and their ways with men.

But like many silent film queens, the Gish sisters in real life were not quite what they seemed on the screen. Neither innocent nor fragile, they had already knocked about the theatrical world for almost a decade, playing children's parts in road companies. They joined the movies in 1912, when Lillian *(at left in the photograph)* was 16 and Dorothy 14, after discovering that a friend, another child actress named Gladys Smith *(below),* was earning $175 a week at Biograph and riding around in a limousine.

The Gishes were unruffled by Biograph's unorthodox screen test, an unnerving 10 minutes during which the director, D. W. Griffith, chased them around the studio with a revolver, shooting off blanks. They signed up at five dollars a day and plunged into an arduous dawn-to-dusk work schedule that included frequent hardship and even danger. In one movie, *Way Down East,* Lillian was sent floating down Connecticut's Farmington River on an ice pack, clad in a thin dress, her arm trailing in the frigid water, for more than 100 takes. Her prescription for surviving such ordeals was a regimen of spartan self-discipline: "Don't eat much, take calisthenics every morning, sleep out of doors, take plenty of cold baths."

Both sisters won kudos for acting; but Lillian achieved the greater acclaim for her outstanding work in *The Birth of a Nation, Intolerance* and *Hearts of the World.* After her performance as a slum waif in *Broken Blossoms,* the theater critic George Jean Nathan rhapsodized, "The smile of the Gish girl is a bit of happiness trembling on the bed of death; the tears of the Gish girl are the tears that old Johann Strauss wrote into the rosemary of his waltzes."

THEDA BARA *(overleaf)* was evil incarnate to millions of movie-goers. Fatally alluring, with death-white face, snaky black hair and sensuous, heavy-lidded eyes, she seemed born to trap unwary males. Rumored to be the daughter of a French painter and his Egyptian mistress, her name was an anagram for "Arab Death." She seemed to personify the wicked siren she played in almost 40 movies, beginning in 1915 with *A Fool There Was,* an adaptation of a Rudyard Kipling poem called "The Vampire."

Privately, Theda Bara was a demure young lady named Theodosia Goodman, daughter of a respectable tailor from Cincinnati, Ohio. Her main ambition was to be known as a conventional romantic heroine. But her one big attempt at sweetness and light, *Kathleen Mavourneen* in 1919, was a resounding flop. For the Hollywood publicity machine, which had been the sole progenitor of Theda Bara's sinister personality, could not undo the spell it had cast over the public. To movie-goers, Theda Bara was "The Vamp" and could not possibly be anything else.

MARY PICKFORD, born Gladys Smith and known to the world as "America's Sweetheart," was the sharpest business head in the movie industry. Despite her shy, sweet smile and cascades of ringlets *(page 61),* she was the acknowledged life master in Hollywood's cutthroat game of salary jumping. Her trump card was a public following that bordered on idolatry. Movie-goers just could not get enough of this coy young maiden, whose age—disguised by careful lighting, a curling iron, and outsized sets designed to make her look even smaller than she really was—seemed fixed at a perennial 16 years.

Mary's Pollyanna charm extended to her dealings with tight-fisted employers. She cajoled her first raise from D. W. Griffith, her director at Biograph, by complaining that several people had recognized her on the subway. "If I'm going to be embarrassed that way in public," she reportedly said, "I'll have to have more money." Her next employer, Adolph Zukor, broke down under the touching plea that "for years I've dreamed of making $20,000 a year before I was twenty. And I'll be twenty very soon now."

THE VAMP

AMERICA'S SWEETHEART

Merry Madcaps at the Fun Factory

On a hot August day in 1912, a special kind of organized mayhem appeared in Hollywood in the form of the Keystone Film Company. This motley troupe of comic actors happened to arrive, according to a famous Hollywood myth, on the day of the town's annual parade of Shriners. Keystone's director, Mack Sennett, seized the opportunity: he sent his star comedienne, Mabel Normand, clutching a baby doll from the dime store, into the ranks of Shriners to look for the child's supposed father. In hot pursuit, Ford Sterling, flapping along in an outsized overcoat, played the part of Mabel's irate, two-timed husband. A brawl erupted between Sterling and an embarrassed Shriner, and the police came charging in to break it up. Meanwhile Sennett, who had set up his camera at curbside, caught the entire ruckus on film and shipped it off to his backers in New York as the first Keystone Comedy.

Ford Sterling, playing a sheriff in "Her Screen Idol," rescues two innocents.

Charlie Chaplin (right), as a British toff, pledges love eternal to a shy maiden.

The promise of marital bliss cannot turn the roving eye of Slim Summerville.

Wallace Beery is hefted off the tracks at the command of Gloria Swanson.

Over the ensuing five years, using precisely this formula of outrageous spontaneity and controlled confusion, Sennett and company cranked out the awesome total of 500 comic shorts. The preposterous Sennett clowns, in baggy pants and giants' shoes, flung hundreds of custard pies and whacked each other with baseball bats in a calculated assault on reason and common sense. Sennett's superbly inept crew of comic policemen, the Keystone Kops, bungled their way through scores of frantic chases, pursuing the bad guys in Tin Lizzies that invariably broke down at railroad crossings in the path of an oncoming express.

Mack Sennett presided over these antics like a master puppeteer. He directed, acted, thought up most of the stories and occasionally even ran the camera himself. He used no scripts, directed according to whim and inspiration, and held story conferences and business meetings while lolling in a bathtub he had installed in his office.

Hollywood dubbed the Keystone studio "the Fun Factory." But out of the mayhem at the Fun Factory emerged almost every great comic star—and many serious actors—of the silent screen, among them (*below and overleaf*): Fatty Arbuckle, Ben Turpin, Wallace Beery, Chester Conklin, Mack Swain, Gloria Swanson and a little man with a twitchy moustache and silly walk named Charlie Chaplin.

A gaggle of bathing beauties sneaks up on Mack Swain and Gloria Swanson.

Chester Conklin woos a damsel on horseback while Louise Fazenda fumes.

Bobby Vernon and Gloria Swanson join hands with Teddy, the Sennett dog.

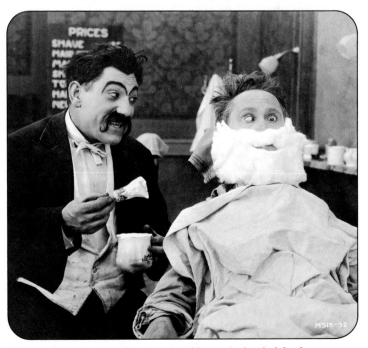

Smothered in lather, Ben Turpin crosses his eyes in dread of the shave to come.

The Keystone Kops uncover a piece of news so dire that Ford Sterling, at the phone, turns rigid in horror and Fatty Arbuckle (right) cannot believe his ears.

Pauline, defiant but overpowered, is bound and gagged by counterfeiters. Luckily, her dog escaped the villains, ran home and led her stepbrother Harry to the rescue.

THE (GASP!) PERILS OF PAULINE

A new kind of movie called the serial hit its stride in 1914 when a sturdy young actress named Pearl White made 20 biweekly installments of *The Perils of Pauline*, sampled on these pages. As Pauline Marvin, an impetuous heiress seeking adventure, she fought off Indians, plummeted from a cliff, drifted off in a runaway balloon, was blown up at sea by a mad pirate, and so on. To the delight of a national audience of *Pauline* addicts, she was saved in the nick of time at the end of each episode by her manly stepbrother and suitor, Harry. The saga inspired a host of thrill-a-minute imitations, including *The Hazards of Helen* and a wild parody called *The Fates and Flora Fourflush*.

Like other early serials, Pauline's encounters with foul play were printed as fiction in local newspapers at the same time they appeared at movie houses. In the single adventure excerpted below, from the *New York American* of May 17, 1914, Pauline plunges into dire trouble when she visits New York's Chinatown with friends, guided by a sinister musician named Signor Baskinelli. The making of this particular episode became painfully realistic when a novice actor, carried away by his part, overdid the fight scene and pummeled Pearl White black-and-blue.

I *am sure you won't disappoint me, Signor Baskinelli. Only the worst and wickedest places."*

He leaned suddenly very near to her. "Do you really mean that, Miss Marvin?" he asked.

"Indeed I do," she answered.

"Would you like to visit the gods themselves?" he asked.

Pauline agreed enthusiastically. "You mean a joss house—a Chinese church, don't you?"

"Yes."

The joss house that most visitors see in Chinatown is the little one at the meeting of Doyers and Pell streets—where men still die silently in the hush of secluded corridors and women vanish into the darkness that is worse than death. But it was not to the little joss house that Signor Baskinelli took his guests. Baskinelli took his guests to the joss house of the Golden Screens.

A light flared behind the door and a Chinaman in American dress admitted them. "I am beginning to be bored," said Pauline.

"Wait; give the wicked a chance," said Baskinelli.

They climbed three flights of dingy narrow stairs and stepped into the dim, smoky presence of the joss.

The joss squatted, six feet high on a block pedestal. One of the peculiar features of the room was a suit of ancient Chinese armor, standing brightly polished beside the statue of the god. A huge two-edged sword of the Samurai was held upright in the steel glove.

"What about it, Baskinelli—better be going?" asked one of the men.

"Yes—yes. I beg only a moment. I wish to show Miss Pauline the—"

"You mean Miss Marvin, do you not?" blazed Harry, striding to Baskinelli's side and glaring down at him. "I want to tell you, you little leper, that if anything happens here tonight—it is going to happen to you." He was so near to him that the others did not hear.

Baskinelli backed away. Pauline, with the swift, inexplicable, yet unerring instinct of women, moved as if to seek the shelter of Harry's towering frame.

He did not see her. He whirled at the sound of the opening of a door. Baskinelli had guided Pauline back to the little door behind the screen. Baskinelli drew aside the curtain. "There—that is one form of adventure."

Pauline looked through the curtain. A suffocating narcotic

Indians insist that their prisoner Pauline help make war against the whites.

Harry begs Pauline not to enter the International Cross Country Auto Race.

odor came to her. What she saw was stifling not only to the senses —but to the soul. She turned away.

"Polly!" Harry's voice rang through the room like thunder.

"We are coming—we are quite safe," called Baskinelli, with the sneer tinge in his tone.

"Very well, then, hurry."

Harry's manner aroused Pauline's temper again. She purposely lingered. Harry had closed the door and followed the others down the outer passage.

"Miss Marvin—Pauline!" called Baskinelli with sudden passion. "Do you know what love is?"

He stepped toward her and tried to take her in his arms. Woman though she was, she was stronger and far braver than he. She thrust him aside and fled through the door. Baskinelli followed, protesting, pleading. Strangely, as she fled through the narrow corridor, the low, flaring gas jets were extinguished one by one. She groped in darkness. Baskinelli's pleading voice became almost a consolation, a protection.

Her elbow struck something in the passageway. The something shrank at the touch. She heard a quick drawn breath that was not Baskinelli's. She knew that she was trapped. She tried to run. The tiny passageway choked her flight. She plunged helplessly between invisible but gripping walls. She reeled and screamed. "Harry! Harry! Come to me!" she cried. She reached the stairs. The stairs were blocked by a closed door. Her weak hands beat upon the wooden panels, helplessly, hopelessly. How should she know that there were two doors, locked and sealed beyond? Her wild screams rang through the long passage. She

On a visit to the West, Pauline is kidnaped by a pair of masked outlaws.

Driven over a tall cliff by a madman, Pauline survives, limp but unscathed.

placed her softly clothed shoulder to the door and strove to break it. She screamed again. "Harry! Harry!"

Dull crashes answered. There was the crack and cleaving of splintered wood. "Hold on! I'm here," she heard.

She fell beside the door. Strong arms seized her. For an instant she felt that she was saved. But she looked up into the lowering face of a man with tilted mustachios. From the wide, thick lips came threats and curses. From the passageway came the crashing of doors. She let herself be lifted, then, with sudden exertion of her trained strength, she broke the grasp of the man. The door fell open. Harry, bloody and tattered, stood there—alone.

"Polly?"

"Oh—yes—where are the others? They'll kill you—run!"

He ran. He ran forward into the black corridor. A knife thrust, sheathed in silence, ripped his shoulder—gave him his cue. He had one man down and trampled. But another was upon him and yet a third. A sharp pain dulled the pulsing of his throat. He felt a trickle down his bared and swinging arm. He fought blindly in the dark. "Polly!" he panted. There was no answer.

In the Joss House of the Golden Screens, the two Chinamen, dazed with opium, set of purpose, were arguing with a trembling priest. The door fell open and a white woman—with bleeding hands—fell at their feet. "Ha, she has come back!" cried one of the Chinese in his own tongue. There was the sound of steps in the outer passage. They lifted Pauline. They dragged her back. The priest hurried to the outer door and locked it. There was the blunt, battering thrust of a powerful body against the door. "Open, or I'll break it in!" yelled the voice of Harry. The priest

Harry rescues his beloved with a breeches buoy from a deserted lighthouse.

After setting a fire, villains disguised as firemen seize Pauline and Harry.

opened the door. In deferential silence he saluted the battle-grimed newcomer. Battered, panting, bleeding, Harry lunged at the man, gripped him. "Quick—where is she? You'll die like a spiked rat. Where?" he roared.

There was a moment's silence, then a strange sound—like a cry from afar off. In a flash, Harry caught from the mailed glove the haft of the sword of the Samurai. He turned in time. Three Chinamen, with drawn knives, were upon him. He swung the unwieldy sword above his head. Its sweep saved him. He dashed at the joss. He struck. The head of the statue thudded to the floor. The Chinese rushed upon him. But he was behind their god, prying open the secret door to the hollow in the statue.

"It's all right, Polly," he said as he drew her gently forth. He stood above her with his back to the wall, swinging the sacred

sword of the Samurai against the onslaught of fanatic men. They fell before him, but more came on. His hands could hardly hold the mighty weapon. For more than half an hour he had been in fight. He was weakening. He braced himself and swung for the last time. There came a hammering at the door. It crashed in. Police clubs whistled right and left. The Chinese fled.

"And I guess that will be all," panted Harry in the taxi that took them home. "I don't think you'll ask for any more adventures after this one."

"Why didn't you pick up the Joss's head?" replied Pauline. "It would have looked so nice and dreadful in the library."

But the glory of Pauline's thick golden hair nestled upon his torn shoulder and Harry knew in his heart that he would go through all the perils in the world for happiness like this.

Set upon by vicious opium addicts in Chinatown, a white-tied Harry fights for his life as Pauline—whose yen for adventure got them into this—watches fearfully.

The splendors of Babylon, re-created for "Intolerance" with plaster elephants and 300-foot walls, were so vast that Griffith had to dangle his camera from a balloon.

"A Sun-Play of the Ages"

The Hollywood movie industry was seldom impressed by the extravagance of its members. But when D. W. Griffith, in 1915 the reigning dean of Hollywood directors, began to construct a huge and fanciful conglomeration of parapets and towers in a lot on Sunset Boulevard, the movie community was agog. Never before had such a monumental set been built, nor had so much expensive talent—a dozen top stars and 15,000 extras—been assembled. What did it mean? What was Griffith, the master, up to now?

The answer came the following year, when a three-hour, $1,900,000 extravaganza called *Intolerance* opened at New York City's Liberty Theatre. The acclaim of critics was overwhelming. "*Intolerance* is so colossal, gorgeous and stunning to the mind that words fail," wrote the *New York Tribune*, and the *New York Evening Post* called it "the highest achievement which the camera has recorded."

But the general public was not so sure. For *Intolerance*, enigmatically subtitled "A Sun-Play of the Ages," was so complex that almost nobody was able to understand it. Its main theme seemed to be an attack on hypocrisy and persecution, worked out in a succession of historical episodes that ranged in setting from ancient Babylonia to

Text continued on page 76.

Griffith shouts orders while his cameraman, Billy Bitzer, adjusts the lens.

MODERN AMERICA

The audience confusion over *Intolerance* arose from Griffith's attempt to weave together four separate stories. The camera would start out showing one episode, then switch in mid-plot to the next. The most poignant of the four stories showed the persecution of two American newlyweds, played by Mae Marsh and Robert Harron *(above)*. Harron, a reformed criminal, was framed by former cohorts and sentenced to death. Only a pardon on the gallows steps *(below)* prevented his execution.

RENAISSANCE FRANCE

Interwoven with the modern story was another tale of persecution and intolerance. It depicted the massacre of French Protestants on St. Bartholomew's Day in 1572, at the instigation of France's Catholic queen, Catherine de Medici. The two lovers, Brown Eyes and Prosper Latour, played by Margery Wilson and Eugene Pallette *(above)*, died in the massacre, while Catherine herself was shown marching triumphantly over the littered bodies of slaughtered Protestants *(below)*.

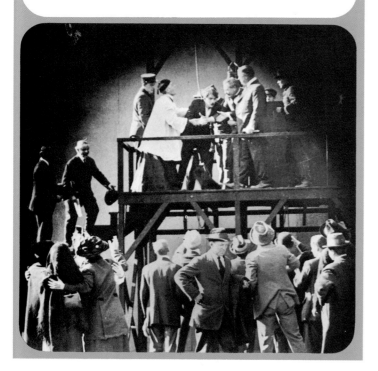

BIBLICAL PALESTINE

As pictorial counterpoint to the other plots, Griffith interspersed scenes from the Crucifixion of Christ. To highlight a tender interlude between the two lovers in the Massacre of St. Bartholomew he showed Christ preaching the gospel of universal love to the people of ancient Palestine *(above)*. To add to the drama of the modern story, he punctuated the innocent husband's march to the gallows by cutting to short scenes of Jesus staggering under the Cross on the way to Calvary *(below)*.

ANCIENT BABYLONIA

Of the four stories, the one that did most to swell *Intolerance* to its colossal proportions was the fall of Babylon to the armies of Persia. Babylon, the sumptuous capital of the ancient world, was conquered and sacked because of a squabble between rebellious priests and King Belshazzar, shown above with his Princess Beloved. The priests, anxious to replace the new state religion with their own, betrayed the city and opened its gates to the invading armies of the Persian tyrant *(below)*.

modern America. But as the scenes flicked on and off the screen in a weird hodgepodge of flashbacks and crosscutting, the result was massive befuddlement. One observer wrote in *Photoplay Magazine,* "The universally-heard comment from the highbrow or nobrow who has tried to get it all in an evening: 'I am so tired.'"

At the box office, the world's first film extravaganza turned out to be a colossal flop. Receipts never came close to balancing the film's gigantic cost, and in 1921 the company that Griffith had formed to produce *Intolerance* was declared bankrupt.

Financial failure did not really bother Griffith. He had been broke before and had managed to pull himself out. The descendant of impoverished Old South aristocrats, he had wandered in and out of professions like a hobo through a train yard, stopping briefly to write plays and poetry, to sell magazine subscriptions and to act in a traveling theatrical company. In 1908 he turned to motion pictures more in sorrow than in hope, joining Biograph simply to earn money. He was so ashamed of being associated with the ignoble occupation of movie-making that he signed his first contract under an assumed name.

For all his embarrassment, Griffith brought the touch of genius to film-making. During five years at Biograph, grinding out one-reel shorts at the rate of two a week, Griffith codified the vocabulary of modern film technique. He perfected such basic devices as the close-up, the long shot, the fade-out and the fade-in. He used his camera like a hawk pursuing a rabbit, zooming in at odd angles to focus on an actor's face, intensifying the emotional impact of a scene with a glimpse of an angry glance, a quivering lip or a falling tear. At times he would plunge parts of the screen into complete darkness, spotlighting only a single important detail, such as a murder weapon or a touching vignette of a mother and child. "The task I'm trying to achieve is above all to make you see," he said.

As Griffith's reputation grew, so did his ambition. In 1914 he decided to form his own film company, the Epoch Producing Corporation, in order to create the immensely successful film that led him to *Intolerance*. The

prototype of the Hollywood blockbuster, this was the epic, *The Birth of a Nation*, which Griffith unabashedly proclaimed was to be the greatest motion picture ever made.

In many ways, it was. *The Birth of a Nation* was also one of the most controversial. A three-hour saga on the Civil War, it traced the devastation of the South and the humiliating aftermath of Reconstruction. Audiences whose grandfathers had fought at Gettysburg and Shiloh watched the horrors of the conflict re-created on the screen. They also watched as Griffith, whose father had been a Confederate colonel, showed with implicit approval and delight the lynching of Negroes and the rise of the Ku Klux Klan.

An aroused public stormed movie theaters, both to see the film, which by the end of the decade grossed an estimated $10 million, and to protest its racist themes. Riots broke out in cities throughout the North, Negro demonstrators marched on the Boston State House and prominent Negro and white leaders demanded that the film be suppressed. President Charles Eliot of Harvard, who apparently felt that an actual viewing of the film was not really necessary, announced, "I have not seen this play, but I want to say that it presents an extraordinary misrepresentation of the birth of this nation."

Griffith was hurt by the furor he had caused. He answered his attackers with a bitter pamphlet on his right to free speech and demanded "the liberty to show the dark side of wrong that we may illuminate the bright side of virtue."

But Griffith's major defense of himself and his art was his next big movie, which was, of course, *Intolerance*. And though it left him broke and led to both confusion in the audience and some outlandishly sentimental scenes on the screen, *Intolerance* was indeed Griffith's artistic masterpiece. A whole generation of Hollywood directors would try to equal the film in spectacle and extravagance. Its battery of technical achievements was plagiarized and imitated by directors from Rome to Moscow, and in 1919 a copy of the film itself was officially purchased by the Soviet government as a pictorial textbook in movie art.

In the grandiose finale of Griffith's great film, soldiers throw down their weapons while a host of angels proclaims the triumph of love over intolerance.

THE CRITICS DRAW A BEAD ON MOVIES

As the motion picture emerged as major entertainment, films came under the scrutiny of a new breed of instant expert: the movie critic. Though these paid observers tended to be overly harsh toward the popular run of Hollywood art (e.g., *The Perils of Pauline* and the Sennett comedies), they often erred the other way in praising some of the melodramas that the studios spooned out. To be sure, films such as D. W. Griffith's *Broken Blossoms (overleaf)* or individual performances on the order of John Barrymore's in the dual role of Dr. Jekyll and Mr. Hyde did indeed deserve their raves. On other occasions, however, the critics seemed under some mystical spell from the studios. It took no small measure of positive thinking, for example, for a critic to praise straight-facedly a corpulent Elmo Lincoln as Tarzan heaving unfriendly explorers around the African jungle. And it required a high degree of self-hypnosis to find unbroken grandeur in some of the scruffy sets of Cecil B. deMille's melodrama, *Male and Female*, starring Gloria Swanson and Thomas Meighan. Even the poet Vachel Lindsay, who early on recognized the artistic potential of the new medium, let his enthusiasm carry him to bewildering flights of theoretical analysis. Reviewing the role of cinematic cowboy as practiced by William S. Hart—shown at right, with friends, earnestly holding the bad guys at bay—Lindsay galloped off into the thick smoke bank of hypothesis, excerpted below.

As the crowd blocked his retreat, Hart jumped his horse through the window with much crashing of glass. He dragged the pair after him, producing an acute example of the type of tableau I call Sculpture-in-motion. Later, when the pony is chasing the train and is nearest to the camera, it is, in a primitive way, Sculpture-in-motion. But when the end of the train fills the screen, we have architecture. It has a roof, walls, a floor, windows, door, chairs, and inhabitants, and it is certainly in motion. Above all, it is the leading actor in this episode. This is the principle of Architecture-in-motion.

NEW REPUBLIC, 1917

"BROKEN BLOSSOMS"

When the incomparable Lillian Gish creeps into the soul of the poor little cockney child of a prize fighter, it's more than the heart can endure. The child is used by the father to vent his rages. A Chinaman sees her exquisite loveliness and worships her. One day she falls at his doorway after one of her father's brutal attacks, and for the first time she learns what tenderness and kindness is. But the father finds where she is, drags her home and he whips her for the last time, and the little blossom is broken and dies.

OHIO STATE JOURNAL, 1919

"TARZAN OF THE APES"

"Tarzan of the Apes," with Enid Markey and Elmo Lincoln, is above all else different, wherein its success should lie. We are, all of us, tired of looking at society, sex, allegorical and historical pictures, and it is a relief to view a picture with a unique jungle story, in which the hero is kidnapped as a child by apes and brought up by them. Add some exciting jungle scenes, apes in great quantity, the appearance in jungleland of Jane Porter in the person of Enid Markey and you have a close-up of "Tarzan of the Apes."

THEATRE MAGAZINE, 1918

"MALE AND FEMALE"

It is a typical Cecil B. deMille production—audacious, glittering, intriguing, superlatively elegant and quite without heart. It reminds me of one of our great California flowers, glowing with all the colors of the rainbow and somehow devoid of fragrance. The glorious Gloria Swanson is quite literally uncovered to view. In the moments when the soul of a woman is almost but not quite born in the tigerish and silken body, Miss Swanson does not particularly impress, but at all times she is assuredly an eyefull.

PHOTOPLAY MAGAZINE, 1919

"ROMEO AND JULIET"

"Romeo and Juliet" is genuinely entertaining, colorful, and competently played as presented by Francis X. Bushman and Beverly Bayne. Bushman, we should say, is not a great Romeo. He fails to wring the sympathy. But how he looks the romantic hero! The bucko probably will be taken most by its swashbuckling action. The literati should find pleasure in the fact that the scenario man did not attempt to rewrite Shakespeare. And the romantic girl, no doubt, will go dotty over the sentimental aspect.

CLEVELAND LEADER, 1916

"DR. JEKYLL
AND
MR. HYDE"

I went to see John Barrymore in "Dr. Jekyll and Mr. Hyde," and it would give the wrong impression to use the slang of the moment and say that it left me cold. However, that literally was true. I felt chilled. It was as if I had stepped on ice with my bare feet. Dollars to doughnuts you'll feel the same way. It is that strange paradox, one of the most hideous, ugly and haunting things imaginable; and one of the most artistic and beautiful dramatic pictures that it has been my privilege to see. John Barrymore, by means of the screen, makes both men, Jekyll and Hyde, possible males. Jekyll is so thoughtful of others that he is called "the St. Anthony of London." On the other hand, Barrymore's Hyde visualizes the evil that is in every man, it shows the collective evil of the male.

I must admit that the praises have not been too loud for young Mr. Barrymore. And it's strange, perhaps, that it took the motion pictures to bring about a full realization of his greatness. Now I am willing to believe that we have not another actor on the American stage who ranks with him, all points considered. Here is great acting. "Dr. Jekyll and Mr. Hyde" is a great picture. Awful in its intensity; sublime, however, in its artistry.

CLEVELAND *PLAIN DEALER*, 1920

The Tin Lizzie

Model Ts await repairs at the Ford garage, a fixture of every town.

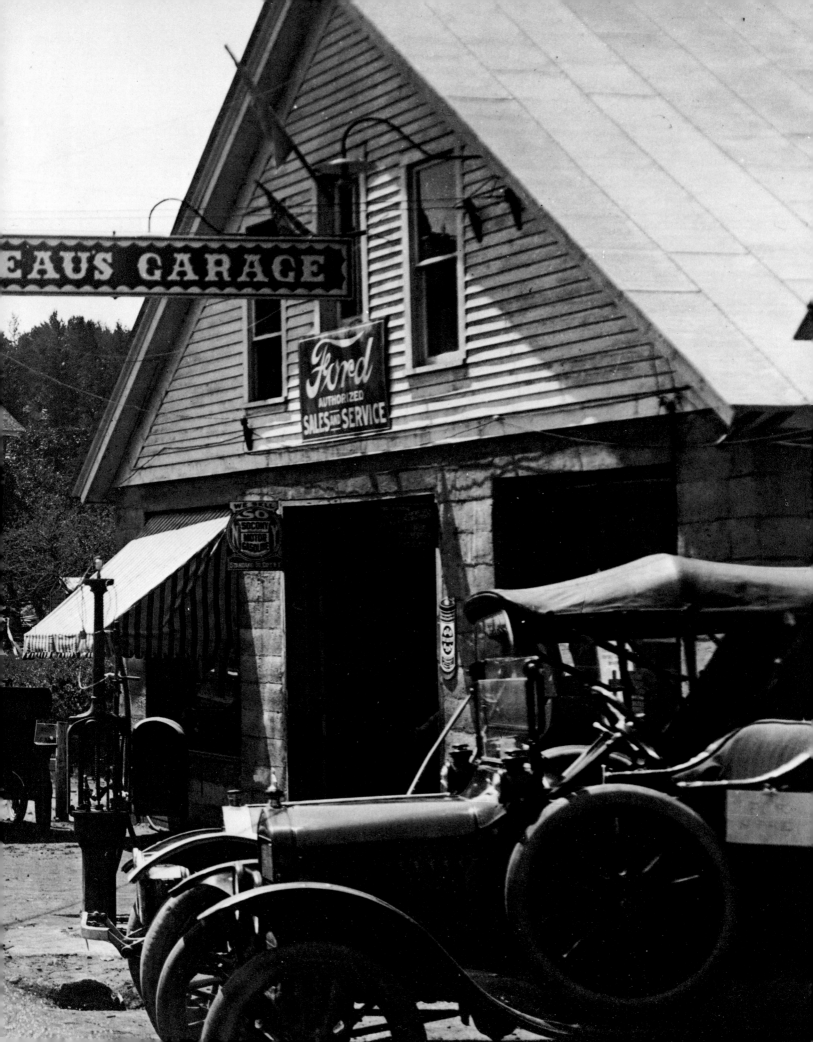

The Homely Vehicle That Changed America

The way to make automobiles is to make one automobile like another automobile,
to make them all alike, to make them come through the factory just alike.

HENRY FORD

On the eve of the century's second decade, the automobile industry was struggling to get into high gear—if indeed high gear existed. True, Americans were flocking to auto shows to admire such luxurious chariots as the Pierce Arrow or the Welch Tourer, but most people went only as lookers. One newspaper, assuming only the rich could afford cars, advised that former coachmen made the best chauffeurs because they could be counted on to know "exactly what is expected of them by their masters."

Then in 1908 a self-taught engineer named Henry Ford came out with an auto designated the Model T, which he boldly advertised as "The Universal Car." On first sight, Ford's new baby looked like a creation only a father could love—flat-nosed, all angles and bolts and knock-kneed awkwardness. But once Henry's homely child hit the road, it ran circles around the competition, whisking with ease over the muddy, rock-strewn byways that crisscrossed the nation. With the proper attachments, the versatile T also proved able to handle such back-country chores as pumping water, plowing fields and generating electricity.

Affectionately nicknamed the flivver, Tin Lizzie or just plain "she" by her growing army of buyers, the Model T was the object of a special kind of exasperated love. Fliv-ver owners noted that the tendency of the fenders to soften and wrinkle was a good thing because it allowed the car to get in and out of tight spots. If the car seemed pokey, they tossed into the gas tank camphor balls, which were supposed to pep up performance; or if fuel costs were running high, the flivver might be fed a cheap solution of kerosene and old candle ends. The Model T was such a rudimentary mechanism that almost any handy male could fix it, given a bare-bones tool kit of a wrench, ball-peen hammer, screw driver and some heavy wire. To assist the home mechanic, Ford thoughtfully provided replacement parts like mufflers at 25 cents apiece and a whole new fender for only $2.50. But for such frills as windshield wipers and rearview mirrors, the car owner had to turn to outside entrepreneurs catering to what Ford considered hedonism on the part of some customers.

By the end of the decade, the homely Tin Lizzie had indeed blossomed into the universal car. Nearly four million of them, all nearly alike as Ford had said they should be, were rattling around the country; and by providing more or less instant transportation for the mass of American people, they were transforming a horse-and-buggy land of isolated villages into a mobile, modern nation.

Standing seven feet tall, the spindly and awkward-looking Model T proved to be durable and agile on the road. In 1911 the wooden body was replaced by metal.

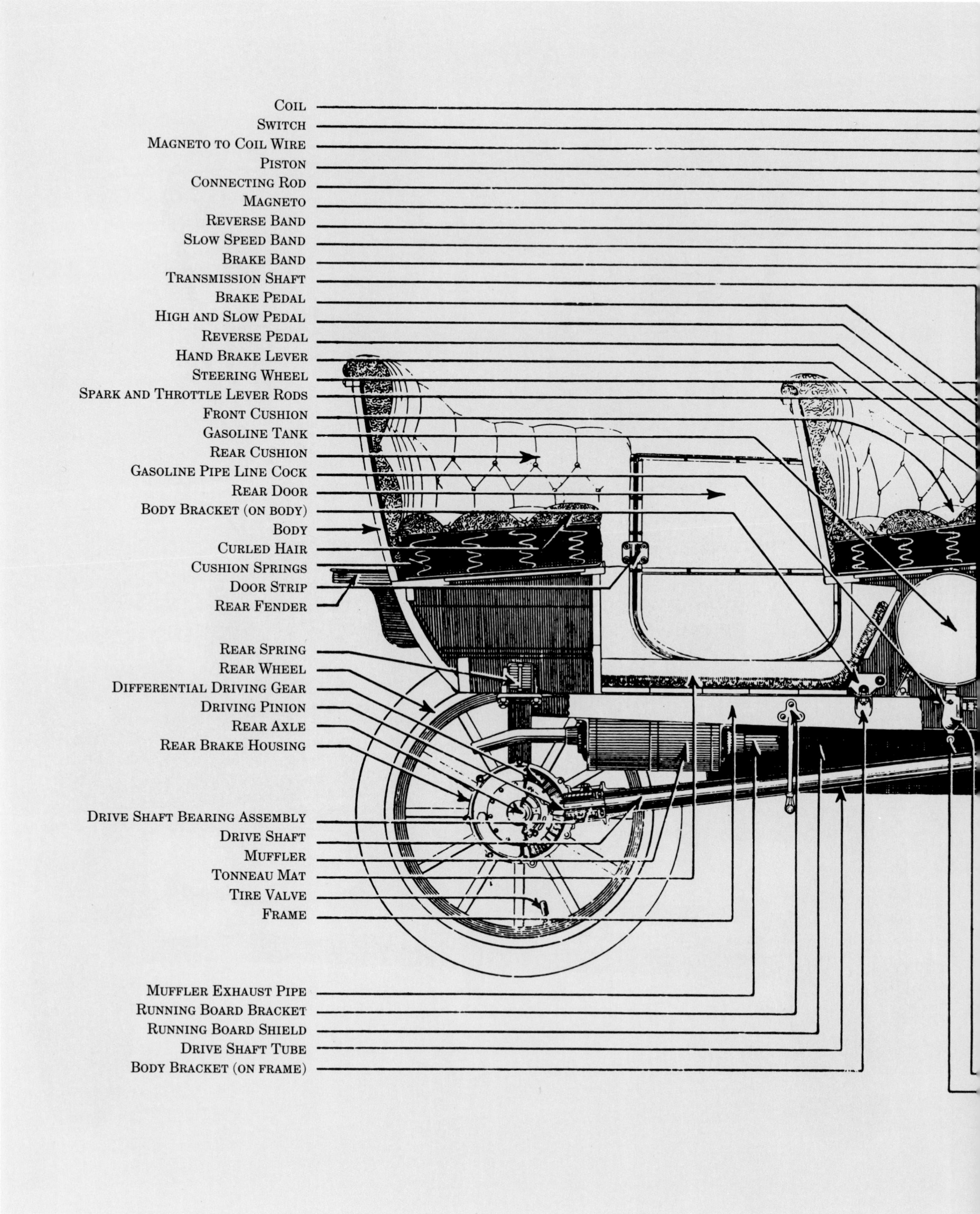

COIL
SWITCH
MAGNETO TO COIL WIRE
PISTON
CONNECTING ROD
MAGNETO
REVERSE BAND
SLOW SPEED BAND
BRAKE BAND
TRANSMISSION SHAFT
BRAKE PEDAL
HIGH AND SLOW PEDAL
REVERSE PEDAL
HAND BRAKE LEVER
STEERING WHEEL
SPARK AND THROTTLE LEVER RODS
FRONT CUSHION
GASOLINE TANK
REAR CUSHION
GASOLINE PIPE LINE COCK
REAR DOOR
BODY BRACKET (ON BODY)
BODY
CURLED HAIR
CUSHION SPRINGS
DOOR STRIP
REAR FENDER

REAR SPRING
REAR WHEEL
DIFFERENTIAL DRIVING GEAR
DRIVING PINION
REAR AXLE
REAR BRAKE HOUSING

DRIVE SHAFT BEARING ASSEMBLY
DRIVE SHAFT
MUFFLER
TONNEAU MAT
TIRE VALVE
FRAME

MUFFLER EXHAUST PIPE
RUNNING BOARD BRACKET
RUNNING BOARD SHIELD
DRIVE SHAFT TUBE
BODY BRACKET (ON FRAME)

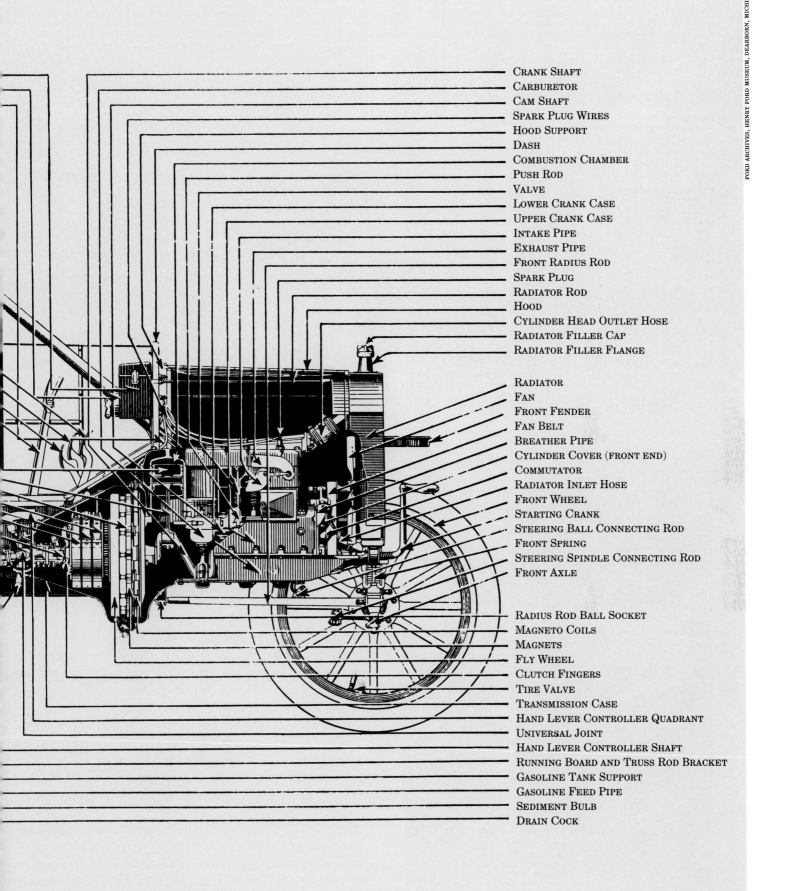

CRANK SHAFT
CARBURETOR
CAM SHAFT
SPARK PLUG WIRES
HOOD SUPPORT
DASH
COMBUSTION CHAMBER
PUSH ROD
VALVE
LOWER CRANK CASE
UPPER CRANK CASE
INTAKE PIPE
EXHAUST PIPE
FRONT RADIUS ROD
SPARK PLUG
RADIATOR ROD
HOOD
CYLINDER HEAD OUTLET HOSE
RADIATOR FILLER CAP
RADIATOR FILLER FLANGE

RADIATOR
FAN
FRONT FENDER
FAN BELT
BREATHER PIPE
CYLINDER COVER (FRONT END)
COMMUTATOR
RADIATOR INLET HOSE
FRONT WHEEL
STARTING CRANK
STEERING BALL CONNECTING ROD
FRONT SPRING
STEERING SPINDLE CONNECTING ROD
FRONT AXLE

RADIUS ROD BALL SOCKET
MAGNETO COILS
MAGNETS
FLY WHEEL
CLUTCH FINGERS
TIRE VALVE
TRANSMISSION CASE
HAND LEVER CONTROLLER QUADRANT
UNIVERSAL JOINT
HAND LEVER CONTROLLER SHAFT
RUNNING BOARD AND TRUSS ROD BRACKET
GASOLINE TANK SUPPORT
GASOLINE FEED PIPE
SEDIMENT BULB
DRAIN COCK

The Ford Motor Company offered customers this cross-section of the utilitarian Model T on the theory that "the better you know your car the better you will enjoy it."

The seven stages of transportation

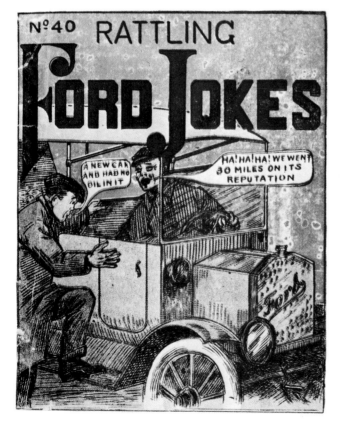

"The jokes about my car sure helped to popularize it," Henry Ford once said; "I hope they never end." For a good part of the decade, the flood of Ford jokes indeed seemed unstoppable. In fact, the commentary about Henry Ford's ubiquitous product was as much a part of everyday conversation as discussion of politics or the weather. Toastmasters and vaudeville monologuists could get a guaranteed laugh by taunting the T; doctors cheered up their patients with quips about the flivver; preachers leavened their sermons with an occasional Ford joke—and skeptics could retaliate with the comment that the Model T "has shaken hell out of more people than that evangelist Billy Sunday ever saw."

The jibes were compiled in paper-bound booklets *(left)* and hawked by boys who wandered up and down the aisles of trains crying, "Peanuts, oranges, candy, cigars and Ford joke books—two hundred good jokes for only fifteen cents." College students pasted labels on their flivvers saying, "Danger, 100,000 jolts" or "Come on, baby, here's your rattle." Occasionally there were some kindly comments on the Model T's redeeming virtues, such as its remarkable ability to get through the mud. Mostly, however, the flivver was the butt of good-natured disparagement.

FARMER—"HUH! FELLER COME ALONG HERE 'BOUT AN HOUR AGO ALL RIGHT—WITH A 'FORD'"

A man on his deathbed had one final request to make—that his flivver be buried with him, because "he had never been in a hole yet where his Ford didn't get him out."

A man pulled in to a filling station and requested a pint of gasoline. The attendant suggested that perhaps he should buy a bit more fuel. "No," said the man, "I don't want to give it any more. I'm weaning it."

"I hear they are going to magnetize the rear axle of the Ford."
"What's the idea?"
"So it will pick up the parts that drop off."

After all, the Ford is the best family car. It has a tank for Father, a hood for Mother, and a rattle for Baby.

"I understand you have just bought a Ford."
"Yes, I saw seven of them chasing one pedestrian the other day, and I decided that I was on the wrong end of the sport."

The guy who owns a secondhand flivver may not have a quarrelsome disposition, but he's always trying to start something.

"My job," said a garbage man, "is getting harder every year. Dead cats is bad enough, an' broken bottles is hell, but the worst on the temper and the fingers is sortin' out them damn little Fords."

"He named his Ford after his wife."
"How funny!"
"Not at all. After he got it, he found he couldn't control it."

"Can I sell you a speedometer?"
"I don't use one. When my Ford is running five miles an hour, the fender rattles; twelve miles an hour, my teeth rattle; and fifteen miles an hour the transmission drops out."

"Have you heard the last Ford story?"
"I hope so."

Minutes after plunging into a ditch, this hardy flivver was able to proceed on its way, undamaged—thanks to Ford's use of the strongest steel frames in any car.

The owner of a stalled flivver gets a bit of exercise trying to crank four cylinders to life. Once the Model T got rolling, it could do 40 miles per hour on a flat stretch.

The ascension of three flights of steps in Duluth wins a $100 wager for one T-owner.

A Ford dealer in Ohio proves the flivver's prowess by carrying 50 passen

As advertised, a Model T was stronger and easier to maintain than a horse, and could be jacked up and used for a myriad of chores, such as grinding grain (above).

The adaptability of the T never ceased to delight the public; this bus for tourists was welded together from parts of two cars by an ingenious Florida mechanic.

A city family picnics near the flivver after a drive to the country. Although not one to sniff at urban sales, Ford most cherished the success of his car with farmers.

Humanity's Sometime Friend

A song of the decade called "Flivver King" provided a tuneful summation of the popular fascination not only with the Tin Lizzie but with the homespun genius who made the marvelous little auto:

Henry Ford was a machinist,
He worked both night and day,
To give this world a flivver,
That has made her shivver,
And speeded her on her way.
Now he is a billionaire,
But his record is fair,
He is humanity's friend.

There was no arguing with most of those thoughts. Henry Ford was unquestionably a machinist, quite possibly the greatest the world had ever known. An inspired, compulsive tinkerer with an uncanny nose for market trends, by 1914 he had burst ahead of Detroit's young pack of auto makers as the master builder in a business that was fast becoming the biggest in the world. In that year his factory turned out the awesome total of 240,700 cars—almost as many as all other automobile companies combined.

Ford would soon share the title of "billionaire"—usually pronounced in an uncomprehending whisper—with John D. Rockefeller and Andrew Mellon. But while Rockefeller and Mellon had reached that rarefied height by complex financial juggling in far-flung oil, and diverse holdings in banks, steel, and coal, Henry Ford stuck close to the script of the American Dream. He built the very best mousetrap in the land—the Model T—and he priced it within reach of almost everybody. The same flivver that could be bought for $850 in 1908 went for $360 eight years later. To baffled competitors, who could not comprehend Ford's apparent refusal to rake in maximum profits, Henry stated, as if it were the most obvious thing in the world, "Every time I lower the price a dollar, we gain a thousand new buyers."

The production of ever cheaper Model Ts would have been impossible if their creator had not devised an equally revolutionary manufacturing method. In most automobile factories, versatile mechanics toted parts from stock piles to stationary chassis, which they assembled from the ground up. Ford perfected a system of line production that required little motion and less skill. Furnaces and drills and lathes were sequentially arranged to make the parts with the fewest possible interruptions; feeder lines then carried the parts to workers who installed them on each incomplete vehicle as it "flowed" past on a chain-driven assembly line. Around the world, this mass production system would soon be called "Fordism."

Despite such industrial heroics, in 1914 Ford's name was still not even listed in *Who's Who in America.* Perhaps many of the more lily-handed financiers of democracy's peerage would have preferred things to stay that way. For, unlike other newly rich men who craved to assume an aura of aristocracy, Henry Ford was first and always a mechanic; he loved nothing better than rolling up his sleeves and fiddling with gears or engine parts until his hands were coated with grease. His mechanical skills were legendary in Detroit. When faced with a problem of distribution of weight or adjustment of components, he solved it by sheer inspiration and often left more scientific minds far behind. Defending a decision, he once said, "Well, I can't prove it, but I can smell it."

Ford had no use whatever for the search for knowledge that seized so many aspirants to culture in the decade *(pages 106-139).* "Books muss up my mind," he said. Taking the offensive on another occasion, he stated, "I don't know much about history, and I wouldn't give a nickel for all the history in the world. History is more or less bunk."

Thus armored against ideas that contradicted his own, he prepared to sally forth into the great world beyond the automobile industry. Many ideas for the improvement of mankind were incubating in his mind during his quiet climb to great wealth. And by 1914, despite the omission from *Who's Who,* he finally was becoming big enough to be heard in matters beyond the boundaries of pure mechanical production. In a typically brash, though inspired, move, he seized the attention of the nation by announcing that the Ford Motor Company would "initiate the greatest

Ford's main ambition, according to a friend, was "to be known as a thinker of an original kind," and he often retreated to the countryside for long periods of meditation.

revolution in the matter of rewards for its workers ever known to the industrial world." What followed was worthy of the fanfare. Ford doubled his workers' pay from an average wage of $2.34 to $5 per day and at the same time reduced the nine-hour shift to eight hours. This extraordinary gesture, announced at a time when the country was in the throes of a depression, made Ford into a folk hero. The New York press devoted 52 columns to the story. In the words of the *Sun*, "It was a bolt out of the blue, unheard of in the history of business." Predictably enough, one well-to-do businessman called Ford "a traitor to his class," and *The Wall Street Journal* weighed in with the comment that the wage hike was a "misapplication of Biblical and spiritual principles in a field where they do not belong."

Suddenly the nation wanted to know all about him. Newspaper reporters, dispatched to Detroit to size up the auto magnate, found Ford to have been cut in the lean, angular, shrewd but slow-talking mold of Abe Lincoln, Davy Crockett and other folk heroes of the past. Here was a genuine industrial tycoon with none of the tycoon's airs: Ford had his wife darn his socks, detested rich men's clubs, avoided social gatherings and refused to employ a butler because he could not bear the idea of a servant standing behind his chair watching him eat. The public was informed, furthermore, that Henry loved birds, often held business conferences outdoors under trees and believed that "the best use I can make of my money is to make more work for more men."

Ford was actually making more work for the men he already had. To meet higher payroll costs, he simply speeded up the production lines, and with his employees working at breakneck pace, he doubled company profits within two years of the announcement of the Five-Dollar Day. Critics soon detected other disquieting fissures in the auto maker's heroic image. Ford, having gained the ear of the public, was not about to give it up. He began to behave like an all-purpose oracle.

The trouble with mankind, as Ford saw it, was that the solid values of small-town America were decaying. If only people would give up alcohol, divorce, gambling, luxury, art, jazz, modern dancing and big cities, the world would be in a far better way. He also believed that granulated sugar was bad because its crystals cut blood vessel walls, and he once stated that all the diseases and evil acts of mankind were due to wrong mixtures of food in the stomach.

A further gall to Henry's hopes for mankind was the laziness that he saw everywhere. "Life is work," he said, "and when work is over, there is nothing to do but wait for death to take you away." Above the fireplace of his home in Dearborn was inscribed the adage, "Chop Your Own Wood and It Will Warm You Twice."

In fact, Ford regarded "The Day's Work" as a sacred code—and a solution to much of the unrest in the world. For example, when the U.S. prepared to send a military detachment to the Mexican border in 1916 to put down roving bands of revolutionaries, Ford said, "If we could put the Mexican peon to work, treating him fairly and showing him the advantage of treating his employers fairly, the Mexican problem would disappear."

No one could deny that Ford gave every evidence of practicing the virtues of hard work that he preached. The trouble was that he insisted, peremptorily, that his employees practice them too. Occasionally a hawk-eyed member of Ford's squad of efficiency experts would lurk behind a production-line worker with a stop-watch, and observe the motions of his arms, hands and fingers. If they detected any waste motions (one hapless worker was found to be making 70,000 unnecessary movements per day), the man would be told how to improve his performance—and no one dared to object.

Efficiency in the factory was not enough, however. Ford wanted efficiency in the home as well, and to this end he created an inquisitional organization called "The Sociology Department." The "sociologists" were agents who interrogated the wife, children and neighbors of a worker to determine if he was "morally fit" for employment by Ford. If the man used alcohol, or was divorced, or quarreled with his wife, or gambled, or owed money, or took

On one of their frequent trips, four famous friends—(from left) Thomas Edison, naturalist John Burroughs, Ford and Harvey Firestone—explore an abandoned mill.

Ford and his wife, Clara, watch birds on their 2,000-acre farm, Fair Lane. *Not one to stand on dignity, Ford has his picture taken with two chums at the zoo.*

A lover of animals, Ford feeds a pet deer. He also raised pheasants on his farm and fed them a diet of custard.

The son of a farmer, Ford displays his still sharp skill at cradling oats during a camping trip in 1918. *Henry II romps with his indefatigable grandfather.*

in boarders or stayed out late at night, he had to correct his ways immediately if he wanted to keep his job. The head of the Sociology Department said: "The impression has somehow got around that Henry Ford is in the automobile business. It isn't true. Mr. Ford shoots about fifteen hundred cars out the back door of his factory every day just to get rid of them. They are but the by-products of his real business, which is the making of men."

After Ford felt reasonably well established in the man-building business around Detroit, he turned his attention to what he considered the most odious flaw in the behavior of mankind as a whole—namely, War. "A habit, a filthy habit," he called it. Ford knew why he detested war; it wasted resources and manpower that rightly should go to the production of material goods. Furthermore, wars were started by the wrong people for all the wrong reasons. In his widely aired opinion, a conspiracy of "International Jews," together with the absentee owners of Wall Street, had instigated the European conflict.

As America came closer and closer to intervention, Ford declared that he would burn his factory to the ground before accepting a single order for cars that might be used for military purposes. He pledged his "life and fortune" to further the cause of peace. A foreign-born pacifist named Rosika Schwimmer took him at his word and asked his help in her plan to transport a delegation of prominent U.S. citizens to Europe, where they would persuade the warring nations to negotiate a truce. Madame Schwimmer was taken aback when Ford repeated to her the conviction that Jews had caused the war (she happened to be Jewish), but she overlooked the comment and managed to convince Ford to hire a ship to carry the pacifists across the Atlantic. He immediately sent invitations to thousands of public figures, asking them to join the mission, but he received uniformly cool replies. Ford then sought President Wilson's endorsement and was rebuffed ("He's a small man," Henry concluded). Next he talked with Cardinal Gibbons in Baltimore and won what he took to be an unqualified blessing for the Peace Ship. The next day, the Cardinal corrected Ford's impression by announcing that he always said "God bless you" at the end of an interview, but that he had little hope for the peace mission. The press began to treat this clumsy statecraft with derision, calling Ford a "rich fool" and a "rustic innocent."

Stung, but unstoppable, Ford chartered a steamer, the *Oscar II.* Fifty-seven reporters joined the boatload of distinctly unprominent pacifists as Ford set out to alter history. On the way over, however, Ford contracted a bad cold. A friend, the Episcopal clergyman Samuel Marquis, took advantage of Ford's depressed state and convinced him that he was on a fool's errand. Ford returned home the minute *Oscar II* touched the opposite shore.

Back in Detroit, he did an abrupt philosophical about-face which left even the most hardened Ford-watchers dumbfounded. Suddenly—and profitably—he became the archpatriot, and committed his factories to all-out production for the war effort. His proposal to build thousands of one-man submarines powered by Model T engines was hooted at by the Navy Department (gasoline engines would not run under water, Ford was informed), but he did manufacture mountains of helmets, airplane motors, trucks and Model T ambulances. He announced to the newspapers that he would turn back all his war profits to the government, but he never did.

At the end of the war, Ford quickly retooled to maintain his dominance of the auto industry, and soon every second motor vehicle in the country was a Model T. He also took time out to fight a personal war with no less an adversary than the *Chicago Tribune.* Back in 1916, when Pancho Villa and his revolutionaries were rampaging in the Southwest, Ford had vigorously opposed sending U.S. troops to the Mexican border. In an editorial the *Chicago Tribune* had called Ford an "ignorant idealist" and an "anarchist," and the indignant auto magnate immediately sued for libel damages of one million dollars. The case finally came to court in 1919 in the small country town of Mt. Clemens, Michigan. It turned into one of the great circus trials of the century.

The *Tribune* lawyers asserted that Ford was indeed an anarchist in the broad sense that he was naïve, stupid and unpatriotic. To prove their point, they called him to the witness stand. Ford's lawyers gripped the table and sweated through such exchanges as the following:

Q: Have there been any revolutions
 in this country?

FORD: Yes.

Q: When?

FORD: In 1812.

Q: One in 1812, eh? Any other time?

FORD: I don't know of any others.

Q: Do you know of any great traitors?

FORD: No.

Q: Who was Benedict Arnold?

FORD: He was a writer, I guess.

Q: You must be thinking of Arnold Bennett.

But in the end, Ford's ingenuous answers earned him the sympathy of the jury, not to mention the millions of newspaper readers who were following the trial. And he had the last word on the matter of history: "I could find a man in five minutes who could tell me all about it."

Ford's performance on the witness stand was perfectly in the image of a true American hero—a hayseed who was smart enough to become a billionaire and who had the good sense to prefer homespun wisdom to slick, citified ideas. The jury ordered the *Tribune* to pay all court costs and awarded Ford token damages of six cents.

This balanced decision brought a decade of miracles and blunders to a fittingly ambiguous conclusion. It was generally recognized that as an industrialist, Henry Ford had few peers; Lord Northcliffe, the British press tycoon, considered him the symbol of American resourcefulness and energy. As an eccentric, he was equally distinguished; his friend Dr. Marquis sadly admitted that "the isolation of Henry Ford's mind is about as near perfect as it is possible to make it." *The New York Times* best summed up Ford's merits and demerits. Apropos of an abortive attempt by Ford to win a seat in the U.S. Senate in 1918, the *Times* stated: "Ford's entrance into the Senate would create a vacancy both in the Senate and in the automobile business, and from the latter Mr. Ford cannot be spared."

Brimming with confidence, Ford stands beside the captain of the "Oscar II" shortly before setting off on his abortive mission to bring an end to the war in Europe.

Culture

Aspiring artists at Provincetown, Massachusetts, ignore the sea to focus on a dowdy model.

Culture

The Lowbrows Meet the Highbrows

We have a public opinion that quakes before the word highbrow as if it denoted a secret sin.   WALTER LIPPMANN

In the second decade the word culture had at least two entirely different meanings for Americans. To most citizens, culture was a kind of prepackaged force for uplifting both the intellect and the spirit. Included within the broad, motherly embrace of this concept were all kinds of things: sentimental—and sometimes sophisticated—magazine illustrations, like those shown on the following pages; inspirational lectures of the camp meeting called the Chautauqua *(pages 130-139)* and even good table manners.

The brows of the people who subscribed to this view of culture were decidedly middle and low. They never doubted the black-and-white distinctions between evil and virtue put forward by 19th Century moralists, but they were willing to accept a few barely contemporary writers like Mark Twain as both edifying and entertaining in just the right—that is, wholesome—way. They read with satisfaction the self-confident statement of purpose by the editors of *American*, a man's magazine: "What we do in the magazine is to stand at the hard places in the road and cry, 'You can come through; you can win.'" They chortled at the deep-dish humor of short-story master Irvin S. Cobb and at the adolescent misadventures of Booth Tarkington's Penrod. And on the Chautauqua circuit they

were wowed by the perorations of William Jennings Bryan who, together with revivalist Harry "Gatling Gun" Fogleman, was master of the program that circuit managers referred to among themselves as the "mother, home and heaven" number.

Far away, on the opposite rim of the national culture gap, was a noisy group of radicals for whom culture had an entirely different meaning. These rebels, among them such fiery, sometimes bitter, intellectuals as Theodore Dreiser, Sherwood Anderson and cigar-smoking poetess Amy Lowell *(page 128)*, saw culture as an avant-garde weapon for liberating the nation from smug, saccharine conventionality. Banding together in bohemian enclaves in the major cities, they wrote free verse, practiced free love and championed a bunch of odd notions like feminism, psychoanalysis, trade unionism and socialism. In the process of throwing down a shocking challenge to accepted mores, this small but enormously talented band of highbrows also created a brand-new and truly American body of writings and art, founded upon protest and dedicated to the outrageous notion that at the "hard places in the road" an overconfident United States had better pause for thought or else face some dire consequences.

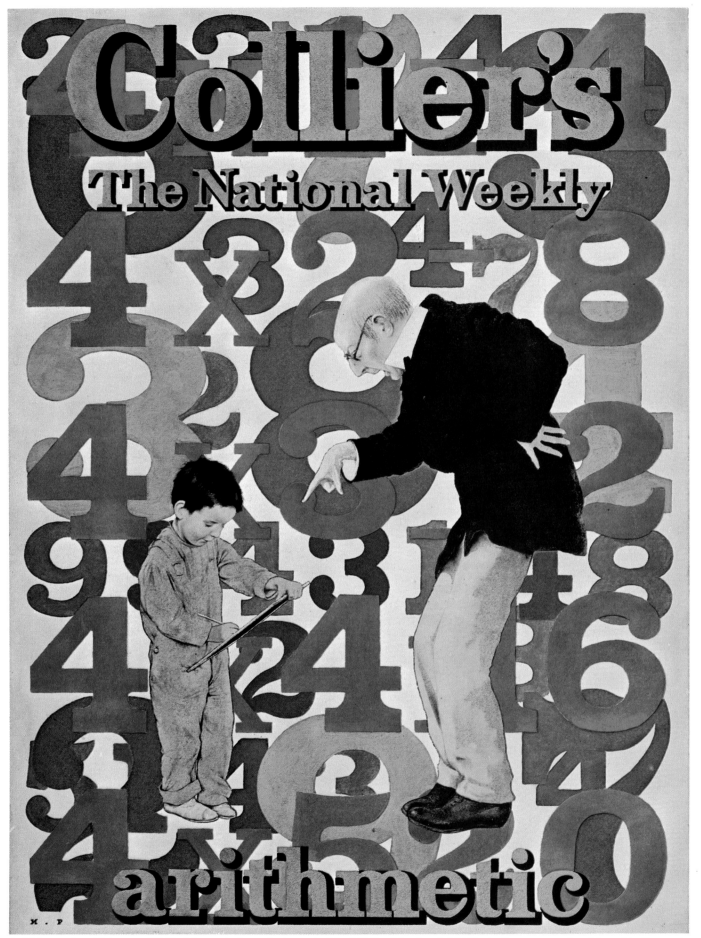

A child struggles with sums on "Collier's" 1911 back-to-school cover by Maxfield Parrish, whose bright illustrations were saved and framed by thousands.

James Montgomery Flagg was renowned for his sentimental style.

Coles Phillips' figures were subtly drawn to blend into the background.

Jessie Smith did scores of "Good Housekeeping" covers of children.

George Plank's fluffy rendering was typical of the stylishness of "Vogue."

THE LADIES' HOME JOURNAL

PAINTED BY HARRISON FISHER

FEBRUARY 1913

FIFTEEN CENTS · THE CURTIS PUBLISHING COMPANY PHILADELPHIA

Harrison Fisher, in a verse to one of his own ideal women, wrote: "She is gentle, she is shy; But there's mischief in her eye, She's a flirt."

THE SATURDAY EVENING POST

An Illustrated Weekly
Founded A... ...8 by Benj. Franklin

MAY 20, 1916   5c. THE COPY

Norman Rockwell

THE EMPIRE BUILDERS—By Mary Roberts Rinehart

Norman Rockwell's first cover for the "Post" showed the penchant for narrative illustration that led him to say, "I am more of a story-teller than painter."

Tops Among the Slicks

Under its motto "The *Post* promises twice as much as any other magazine, and it will try to give twice as much as it promises," *The Saturday Evening Post* presented some of the most popular writers and artists of the decade. Leading all competitors with a circulation of two million in 1913, the *Post* entertained but never shocked its readers with paintings by a promising young illustrator named Norman Rockwell, serials like Harry Leon Wilson's cliff-hanging *Ruggles of Red Gap,* and first-class short stories by Ring Lardner, Edith Wharton, and G. K. Chesterton. Most readers' all-time favorite was Irvin S. Cobb's charming satire "Speaking of Operations," condensed below.

For years I have noticed that persons who underwent pruning at the hands of a surgeon, and survived, liked to talk about it afterward. Of all the readily available topics for use, whether among friends or strangers, an operation seems to be the handiest and the most dependable. It beats the weather, or Roosevelt, or Bryan, or when this war is going to end, if ever, if you are a man talking to other men; and it is more exciting even than the question of how Mrs. Vernon Castle will wear her hair this winter, if you are a woman talking to other women.

Until I passed through the experience myself, however, I never really realized what a precious conversational boon the subject is, and how great a part it plays in our intercourse with our fellow beings on this planet. To the teller it is enormously interesting, for he is not only the hero of the tale but the rest of the cast and the stage setting as well—the whole show, as they say; and if the listener has had a similar experience—and who is there among us in these days that has not taken a nap 'neath the shade of the old ether cone?—it acquires a double value.

"Speaking of operations—" you say, just like that, even though nobody present has spoken of them; and then you are off, with your new acquaintance sitting on the edge of his chair, with hands clutched in polite but painful restraint, gills working up and down with impatience, eyes brightened with desire, waiting for you to pause to catch your breath, so that he or she may break in with a few personal recollections along the same line.

From a mere conversation it resolves itself into a symptom symposium, and a perfectly splendid time is had by all.

Thursday at noon I received from Doctor Z's secretary a note stating that arrangements had been made for my admission into St. Germicide that same evening and that I was to spend the night there. When I woke the young sun was shining in at the window and an orderly dressed me in a quaint suit of pyjamas cut on the half shell and buttoning stylishly in the back, "princesse mode." Then he rolled in a flat litter on wheels and stretched me on it, and covered me with a white tablecloth, just as though I had been cold Sunday-night supper, and we started for the operating room; but before we started I lit a large black cigar, as Gen. U.S. Grant used to do when he went into battle.

Now we were there! They rolled me into a large room, all white, with a rounded ceiling like the inside of an egg. Right away I knew what the feelings of a poor, lonely little yolk are when the spoon begins to chip the shell. Then they put a cloth dingus over my face and a voice of authority told me to breathe. That advice, however, was superfluous and might just as well have been omitted, for such was my purpose anyhow.

But then came another day when I, all replete with expensive stitches, might go forth to mingle with my fellow beings. I have been mingled pretty steadily ever since, for now I have something to talk about—a topic good for any company. "Speaking of operations—" I say. And then I'm off. Believe me, it's the life!

Barometers of Taste

One of the most reliable guides to popular American culture was the bestseller list, a trade barometer dreamed up in 1895 by editor Harry Thurston Peck of the literary review *The Bookman*. The list revealed, for instance, that book buyers were decidedly middlebrow and that an incipient American classic did not necessarily sell. (Sherwood Anderson's *Winesburg, Ohio* sold only a handful of copies when it came out in 1919.) The decade's bestsellers are noted opposite, some with reviews from the period. The top seller in 1916 was the most entertaining of the entire lot: Booth Tarkington's tale of coming of age in small-town America, *Seventeen*, a part of which is excerpted below.

A view of his trousers caused him to break out in a fresh perspiration.

[See page 108.

Chapter 8

*V*oices *from below, making polite laughter, warned him that already some of the bidden party had arrived, and, as he completed the fastening of his third consecutive collar, an ecstasy of sound reached him through the open window—and then, Oh then! It was the voice of Miss Pratt, no less!*

To William's reddening ear Miss Pratt's voice came clearly as the chiming of tiny bells, for she spoke to her little dog in that childlike fashion which was part of the spell she cast.

"Darlin' Flopit," she said, "wake up! Oo tummin' to tea-potty wiz all de drowed-ups. P'eshus Flopit, wake up!"

Dizzy with enchantment, half suffocated, his heart melting within him, William turned from the angelic sounds and fairy vision of the window. He ran out of the room, and the next moment the crash of breaking glass and the loud thump-bump of a heavily falling human body resounded through the house.

Mrs. Baxter, alarmed, quickly excused herself from the tea-table, round which were gathered four or five young people, and hastened to the front hall, followed by Jane. And at a little distance from the foot of the stairs William was seated upon the prostrate "Battle of Gettysburg."

"It slid," he said, hoarsely. "I carried it upstairs with me"—he believed this—"and somebody brought it down and left it lying flat on the floor by the bottom step on purpose to trip me!

I stepped on it and it slid." It seemed important to impress upon his mother the fact that the picture had not remained firmly in place when he stepped upon it. "It slid, I tell you!"

"Get up, Willie!" she urged, and as he summoned enough presence of mind to obey, she beheld ruins other than the wrecked engraving. She stifled a cry. "Willie! Did the glass cut you?"

Some of William's normal faculties were restored to him by one hasty glance at the back of his left leg, which had a dismantled appearance. A long blue strip of cloth hung there, with white showing underneath.

"Hurry!" said Mrs. Baxter.

As for William, he did not even pause to close his mouth, but fled with it open. Upward he sped, unseen, and came to a breathless halt upon the landing at the top of the stairs.

As it were in a dream he heard his mother's hospitable greetings at the door, and then the little party lingered in the hall, detained by Miss Pratt's discovery of Jane.

"Oh, tweetums tootums ickle dirl!" he heard the ravishing voice exclaim. "Oh, tootums ickle blue sash!"

"It cost a dollar and eighty-nine cents," said Jane. "Willie sat on the cakes."

"Oh, no, he didn't," Mrs. Baxter laughed. "He didn't quite!"

"He had to go upstairs," said Jane. And as the stricken listener above smote his forehead, she added placidly, "He tore a hole in his clo'es."

What descriptive information Jane may have added was spared his hearing, which was a mercy.

And yet it may be that he could not have felt worse than he did; for there is nothing worse than to be seventeen and to hear one of the Noblest girls in the world told by a little child that you sat on the cakes and tore a hole in your clo'es.

The Decade's Bestsellers

1911 THE BROAD HIGHWAY *by Jeffrey Farnol: This spicy epic of love lost and love regained in early 19th Century England was said to combine "the spiritual type of swashbuckler adventure with the idyllic tale of the open road."*

1912 THE HARVESTER *by Gene Stratton Porter: In her third tale of life in the swamps of Indiana, the author of "Freckles" created a hero pure of mind and heart "in the hope that a likeness will be seen to Henry David Thoreau."*

1913 THE INSIDE OF THE CUP *by Winston Churchill: No relation to England's First Lord of the Admiralty, St. Louis-born Mr. Churchill related the story of a priest's struggle to comprehend the complex problems of modern life.*

1914 THE EYES OF THE WORLD *by Harold Bell Wright: Supposedly a righteous protest against "patrons of the arts" and artists who prostitute their talents, this work was labeled "pornographic" by a blushing "Boston Transcript."*

1915 THE TURMOIL *by Booth Tarkington: The spokesman for adolescent America turned from light-hearted fare to produce a deeply-felt indictment of a ruthless businessman and "any city, every city, that makes Bigness its god."*

1916 SEVENTEEN *by Booth Tarkington: Back in the world of awkward adolescence, Tarkington told how it was "to be a boy, and seventeen, and in love, and to have a small sister Jane who eats bread spread with apple sauce."*

1917 MR. BRITLING SEES IT THROUGH *by H. G. Wells: After losing a son in the war, Mr. Britling was compelled "to look beyond personal love, beyond the borders of nationalism to find a meaning which would justify the sacrifice."*

1918 THE U. P. TRAIL *by Zane Grey: The joining of East and West by rail was told on "a big canvas, a canvas lurid, volcanic, burnt with human passions at their best and their basest and human energies strained to their tensest."*

1919 THE FOUR HORSEMEN OF THE APOCALYPSE *by V. Blasco-Ibanez: As War, Conquest, Famine and Death laid waste the earth, wealthy ne'er-do-well Julio Desnoyers tangoed his way through life in the bistros of Paris.*

1920 THE MAN OF THE FOREST *by Zane Grey: The theme this time was— can a poor young man accustomed to the solitude of the mountains find happiness as the protector of a young girl of property newly arrived from the East?*

A Hubbub of Highbrows

SHERWOOD ANDERSON

MAX EASTMAN

WALTER LIPPMANN

While most Americans were enjoying lowbrow novels and magazines, a small group of self-styled intellectuals was loudly attacking that banal fare—and a good deal more. In fact the highbrows, among them the writers and editors shown above, demanded nothing less than a cultural revolution. Zealously practicing what they preached, the intellectuals promoted a variety of radical causes and shook up the country with a whole new body of uniquely American literature.

The highbrow revolt found its main strength in middle-class youths recently graduated from Eastern colleges. The rebels from Yale included novelist Sinclair Lewis, class of '08, who published three unsuccessful conventional works before he scored a smashing triumph with his radical satire *Main Street*. Harvard produced the largest crop of highbrows. Van Wyck Brooks, '08, became editor and critic for the avant-garde magazine *Seven Arts*. Walter Lippmann, who had been president of the Harvard Socialist Club in 1909, pursued his political interests, writing provocative books and sophisticated editorials for the radical magazine *New Republic*.

As the revolution spread, it was joined by a number of older men already well established in other careers.

Among the converts were lawyer-poet Edgar Lee Masters and a renegade businessman, Sherwood Anderson, who abandoned his paint factory—and his wife—in favor of fiction writing. Both men shared Lewis' small-town, middle-class background; Masters' *Spoon River Anthology* and Anderson's *Winesburg, Ohio*, like Lewis' *Main Street*, took dead aim on the shortcomings of life in the rural strongholds of old-fashioned mores and morality.

The rebellion came to focus in the big cities, starting with Chicago, where Masters and Anderson set up shop. In point of literary experience the senior member of the Chicago crowd was Theodore Dreiser, whose grim novels were hostile to the good old American values. Two promising poets, Carl Sandburg and Vachel Lindsay, were "discovered" by Harriet Monroe, the staid spinster who edited *Poetry* magazine; she published their blunt, rhythmic works along with those of Ezra Pound and other bright talents in a rising generation of new American poets *(pages 126-129)*. A different sort of female, Margaret Anderson, ran Chicago's second avant-garde magazine, the *Little Review*. Miss Anderson was the consummate bohemian. She wore the very same outfit every day, thrived on a diet of pickles and bread and, for a while, held her lit-

THEODORE DREISER

JOHN REED

FLOYD DELL

erary salon in a tent on the shore of Lake Michigan.

New York, however, boasted such superior cultural resources as book publishers and concert halls, and it gradually captured most of the highbrows. In 1916 New York acquired still another avant-garde attraction, the Provincetown Players. Founded in the Cape Cod resort by vacationing writers and artists, the amateur group rented a theater in Greenwich Village and provided a new outlet for the talents of many highbrows. Among the plays presented were a social melodrama by Harvard man John Reed, who was soon to take part in the Russian Revolution, and *Bound East from Cardiff*, a psychological drama by young Eugene O'Neill. Acting in the plays were such confirmed bohemians as novelist Floyd Dell and Max Eastman, the leftish editor of *The Masses (next page)*. Eastman was a particularly outspoken advocate of the new sexual freedom—so much so that he professed to feel compromised when he got married.

The Players' theater was but one stop on the regular rounds of the Greenwich Village intellectuals. From time to time they would drop in at Alfred Stieglitz' "291 Gallery," which gave the first American showing to such radical modern painters as Pablo Picasso and Henri Matisse. They attended the Liberal Club's costume ball, went to rallies in support of local strikes, turned up in Union Square to applaud the fire-breathing speeches of anarchist Emma Goldman. But their favorite rendezvous was the Fifth Avenue home of wealthy Mabel Dodge.

Mrs. Dodge's drawing room offered food, drink and a platform for radicals of every stripe. Before appreciative audiences of scruffy bohemians, bold suffragettes in "peekaboo" blouses and rich idealists in evening dress, Walter Lippmann talked politics and Edward Arlington Robinson read his deceptively simple poems. Some pungent remarks might be made by Amy Lowell, who was well known as a heavy cigar-smoker, a devoted anthologist of the vivid new Imagist verse and a poet of refined talent. Another frequent guest, much lionized by the highbrows, was the radical labor leader Big Bill Haywood. When that one-eyed roughneck strode into the room, everyone was pleased. Everyone, that is, but a reporter for the conservative *New York Times*, who expressed grave concern about such highly mixed gatherings. He feared that extremist leaders of "the ignorant type" were about to be supplanted by more dangerous "men of education and culture," even by "writers, poets and artists."

A Rebellious Yell from the Avant-Garde

"Hope Springs Eternal—"

This magazine is owned by its editors, has no dividends to pay, and nobody is trying to make money out of it. A revolutionary and not a reform magazine; a magazine with a sense of humor and no respect for the respectable; frank, arrogant, impertinent, searching for the true causes; a magazine directed against rigidity and dogma wherever it is found; printing what is too naked for a money-making press; a magazine whose final policy is to do what it pleases and conciliate nobody, not even its readers.

MAX EASTMAN—EDITOR

Among the leading voices of intellectual revolt during the decade were a clutch of highbrow magazines, with limited circulation but widespread influence in shaping the nation's cultural climate. The most notable of these rather esoteric "little magazines" was a publication with a decidedly proletarian name: *The Masses.* With its tradition-baiting, rabble-rousing editorial policy *(left), The Masses* attracted contributions from the most radical of the country's serious writers and artists.

The Masses was founded in 1911 in New York City's Greenwich Village, capital of the new bohemian intellectuals. It was dedicated, simultaneously, to art, literature, socialism and sheer fun. It paid no money for contributions; the entire editorial budget, in fact, was some $50 a month, divided between its two main editors, Max Eastman and Floyd Dell. But contributions poured in. Such iconoclasts as Walter Lippmann, John Reed and Carl Sandburg used its pages to beat the drum for causes ranging from socialism to free love.

Occasionally, members of the editorial staff wound up in jail in their pursuit of high causes or low comedy. John Reed was arrested for illegal protest while covering a strike of silk workers in Paterson, New Jersey. Another staffer, Ellis O. Jones, was carted off by police for solemnly proclaiming that Greenwich Village had withdrawn from the Union and was now the Free Republic of Washington Square.

Rebellious young artists also combined humor with protest in the magazine's cartoons. The two original art editors of *The Masses,* a kind of Mutt and Jeff of radicalism, were the lanky, petulant John Sloan and Art Young, jovial and corpulent. Young viewed the general conservatism of the decade as "a huge growing belly—progress must pass over it, or blast it, letting the bowels fall where they will." To blast the belly, he and Sloan printed the satirical drawings of such like-minded painters as the young George Bellows and Boardman Robinson. Their cartoons, some of them shown on the following pages, attacked the status quo with a wit and honesty that made *The Masses* a showcase for a fresh and truly American art style.

Ironically captioned "Mid Pleasures and Palaces," this sketch by G. O. Coleman gives a proletarian look to the office of "The Masses" in New York's Greenwich Village.

MEN WANTED FOR THE ARMY MEASUREMENT

ARMY MEDICAL EXAMINER: "At last a perfect soldier!"

Zealously pacifist, "The Masses" attacked the United States' entry into the war with Europe with cartoons such as this piece of mordant satire by Robert Minor.

"WHY DON'T THEY GO TO THE COUNTRY FOR A VACATION?"

Overcrowding of slum streets and tenement buildings was a favorite subject for drawings by George Bellows, a leader in the movement toward social realism in art.

SAVING THE CORPSE

Undertakers wield hypodermics of embalming fluid to defend Tradition, presumably from onslaughts by such radicals as the pioneer abstractionist, Stuart Davis.

RACE SUPERIORITY

Who, exactly, is superior to whom, asks artist John Sloan—the pickaninny with his watermelon or the emaciated white workers shuffling off to their factory jobs?

"You're a Cheap Bunch of Soreheads and You Can't Land Here," says a bloated Uncle Sam in editor Art Young's protest against discriminatory immigration laws.

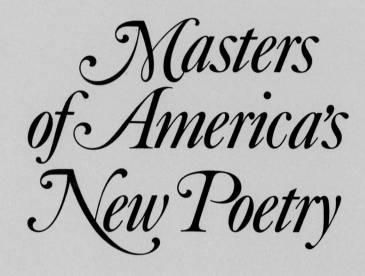

Masters of America's New Poetry

While America's prose writers were clamoring for social and political
reform, a quieter type of revolution was taking place among
the nation's poets. Experimental young bards, such as Carl Sandburg, Vachel
Lindsay, Amy Lowell, Robert Frost, William Carlos Williams
and Edgar Lee Masters (whose works are excerpted in the album on the following
pages) were creating a kind of verse that seemed to flow straight
from the heart. In down-to-earth words and images, they told of things
uniquely American—the grit and muscle of a burgeoning city, the sensations
of apple-picking in a New Hampshire orchard, the fierce emotions
of a Negro revival meeting. Their works spoke so directly to readers that one
collection, Masters' "Spoon River Anthology," chronicling
the hopes and frustrations of ordinary people in a small Illinois town,
became a rare publishing anomaly—a poetic bestseller.

My long two-pointed ladder's sticking through a tree
Toward heaven still,
And there's a barrel that I didn't fill
Beside it, and there may be two or three
Apples I didn't pick upon some bough.
But I am done with apple-picking now.
Essence of winter sleep is on the night,
The scent of apples: I am drowsing off....

AFTER APPLE-PICKING

ROBERT FROST

Hog Butcher for the World,
Tool Maker, Stacker of Wheat,
Player with Railroads and the Nation's Freight
         Handler:
Stormy, husky, brawling,
City of the Big Shoulders....

CHICAGO

CARL SANDBURG

At ten A.M. the young housewife
moves about in a negligee behind
the wooden walls of her husband's house.
I pass solitary in my car.

Then again she comes to the curb
to call the ice-man, fish-man, and stands
shy, uncorseted, tucking in
stray ends of hair. . . .

THE YOUNG HOUSEWIFE

WILLIAM CARLOS WILLIAMS

Lilacs,
False blue,
White,
Purple,
Colour of lilac,
Heart-leaves of lilac all over New England,
Roots of Lilac under all the soil of New England,
Lilac in me because I am New England. . . .

LILACS

AMY LOWELL

A good old negro in the slums of the town
Preached at a sister for her velvet gown.
Howled at a brother for his low-down ways,
His prowling, guzzling, sneak-thief days.
Beat on the Bible till he wore it out
Starting the jubilee revival shout. . . .

THE CONGO

VACHEL LINDSAY

EDGAR LEE MASTERS

Where is Old Fiddler Jones
Who played with life all his ninety years,
Braving the sleet with bared breast,
Drinking, rioting, thinking neither of wife nor kin,
Nor gold, nor love, nor heaven?
Lo! he babbles of the fish-frys of long ago,
Of the horse-races of long ago at Clary's Grove,
Of what Abe Lincoln said
One time at Springfield. . . .

THE HILL

Uplift in Summer

Of all the various cultural vehicles that rolled through America in the second decade, by far the most popular were the inspirational tent shows called Chautauquas. Named after a series of festivals held yearly on Lake Chautauqua in upstate New York, these shows were put together by clever agents, such as the Redpath Bureau in Chicago, and delivered to 40 million Americans every summer in week-long stands in 10,000 towns across the United States. A typical Chautauqua might begin with a rousing band, then offer a series of opera divas, orchestras, magicians, yodelers, Hawaiian crooners, red Indians, and soar to a climax with the inspirational lecturer's passionate exhortation on the glories of personal success.

The people loved it, and everyone from the White House on down had something to say for it. Ex-President Teddy Roosevelt called it "the most American thing in America." Others called it "the great forum of culture and inspiration." And to the home folks, the Chautauqua was not only an opportunity to pick up some packaged enlightenment; it was the social blast of the year.

For weeks in advance of the big event, banners festooned the lampposts all over town; posters studded the tree trunks and shop windows on Main Street; hawkers touted the talent and sold tickets at bargain prices.

Then the great day came. A fresh-painted train emblazoned with the legend of the sponsoring agent chugged into the depot and disgorged the talent. A big brown tent went up at the edge of town—and the show was on.

Queuing up for culture, the folks of Marengo, Illinois, present season tickets at the Chautauqua tent. Redpath, whose banner hangs above, was a major booking agent.

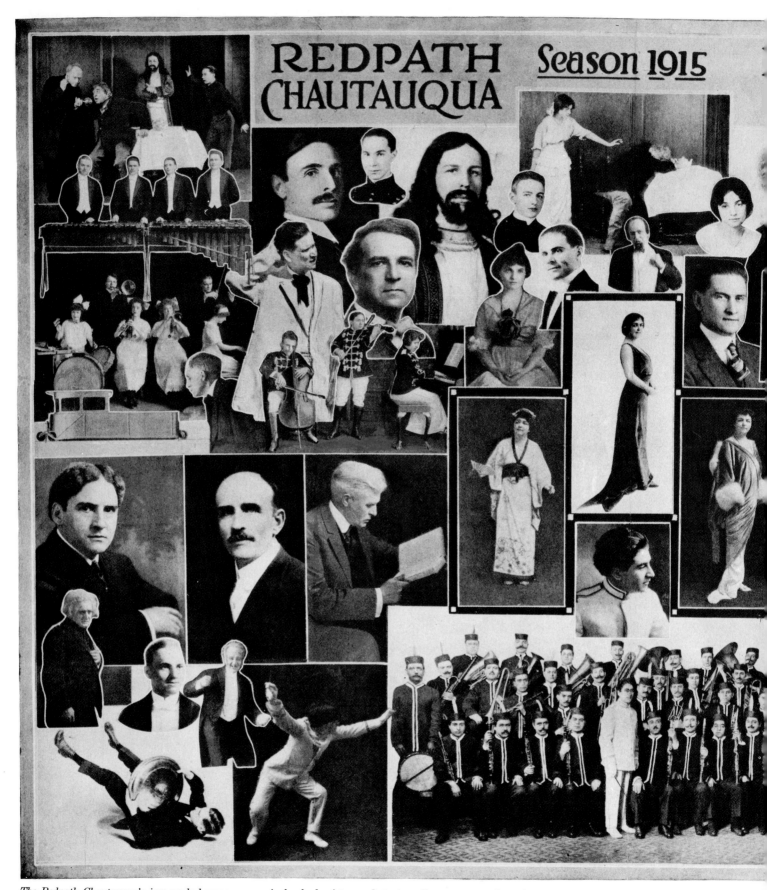

The Redpath Chautauqua's jam-packed program promised xylophonists, acrobats, tragediennes, snappy brass bands and gentlemen orators, all at bargain prices.

The Chautauqua program was a potpourri, but the hit of the show was the inspirational speaker. Redpath's star, Dr. Russell H. Conwell, packed them in with a talk called "Acres of Diamonds" *(excerpted below)*. Its theme was: Make money—which is to be found in your own backyard.

I *say you ought to be rich; you have no right to be poor. I could not find anything better to illustrate my thought than a story I have told over and over.*

There once lived an ancient Persian by the name of Al Hafed. He owned a very large farm with orchards and gardens. One day there visited this old farmer an ancient Buddhist priest, and he sat down by Al Hafed's fire and told that old farmer that if he had a handful of diamonds he could purchase a whole country.

Al Hafed went to his bed that night a poor man—poor because he was discontented. He said: "I want a mine of diamonds!" So he sold his farm and went in search of diamonds.

He wandered into Europe, and at last, when his money was all spent, and he was in rags, wretchedness and poverty, he stood on the shore of that bay in Barcelona, and the poor, afflicted suffering man cast himself into that incoming tide.

Al Hafed's successor led his camel out into the garden to drink, and as that camel put its nose down into the clear water Al Hafed's successor noticed a curious flash of light from the sands, and reaching in, he pulled out a black stone having an eye of light that reflected all the colors of the rainbow.

And thus were discovered the diamond mines of Golconda. Had Al Hafed remained at home and dug in his own cellar or in his garden, he would have had "acres of diamonds"—for every acre, yes, every shovelful of that old farm afterwards revealed the gems which since have decorated the crowns of monarchs.

The Chautauqua served up culture for everybody, including the kids. Here a passel of tots—and some grownups—listen to the Chautauqua's storytelling college girl.

WHITE HUSSAR

POSITIVE THINKER

NOBLE RED MAN

In whatever form they appeared, the Chautauqua acts all oozed health and purity. Typical were the White Hussars, a band of singers resplendent in white uniforms with gold braid, satin-lined capes and white kid boots. Under the baton of director Al Sweet (*above*), they opened all their programs with a rousing "The Boys of the Old Brigade."

Harry "Gatling Gun" Fogleman, so called for his rapid-fire speech, was a former minister who made a fortune peddling positive thinking to the Chautauquas. "A negative thought is a poison as deadly as arsenic," he rattled at 300 words per minute. "Every morning now when I wake up I think positive thoughts and say, 'Fogleman, get out and get to it.' "

By the second decade, the old American r tion that the only good Indian was a dead o had changed to sympathetic admiration f the noble, vanishing red man. Indians li the one above were invited to the Chauta qua, where, decked in feathers and blanket they edified the white man with ancient c emonial dances like the Mating of the Eag

CROONING HAWAIIAN

PROPER MAGICIAN

GOOD GIRL

ardly a Chautauqua program failed to include a Hawaiian feature—a reflection of the rowing interest in the islands. Program otes rhapsodized about the "birds and flowrs, tropic moon, soft murmuring of the aves on the beaches of Waikiki" that were be conjured up by islanders, who plainvely crooned to the tune of their ukuleles.

A magician was as staple an act as a Hawaiian crooner. One often seen was Edwin Brush, who, the program notes said, "will be on every tongue, his tricks the subject of discussion for weeks." And unlike many a Mephistophelian practitioner of the art, Mr. Brush, the notes added, was "a Christian gentleman well worth the knowing."

The Chautauqua opened its platform—and thus new pastures—to the ladies. This welcome did not extend to the usual type of stage actress, who was too racy. Circuit shows tended to feature college girls, who were as wholesome as homemade bread. The lassie above appeared with a group billed as "Walter Eccles and the Four College Girls."

Their eyes fixed in rapt attention, graybeards throb to the Chautauqua climax, an inspiring exhortation to live the good life and make a pile of money.

A New York family poses in a favored American setting—summer at the lake.

America Sits for Its Portrait

The land and the people hold memories; they keep old things that never grow old.

CARL SANDBURG

By the start of the second decade, the camera was just old enough to have become reliable, understandable and compact. Yet it was still new enough to be exciting. Armed with a fast-growing array of equipment, both for stills and movies, journeymen photographers like those at right traveled the Main Streets looking for subjects, and photo studios multiplied. In peaceful Cooperstown, New York, Washington G. Smith and his successor, Arthur J. Telfer, ran such a studio. They investigated almost every aspect of village life for 100 years, and left behind 60,000 pictures of which four, taken during this decade, appear on pages 140-141, 148, 149 and 152-153. Other photographers, very like Smith and Telfer, preserved an indelible record of their own hometowns.

The opportunities for amateur photographers were just as rich. For the camera itself had become democratized to the point where virtually any American could own and use one. George Eastman noted in 1913 that "the first Kodak was sold for $25.00. At the present time a camera much better in every respect except the covering of the case is sold for $2.00." For a mere six dollars, the picture-taker could arm himself with something even more new and exciting: a folding, pocket-sized Autographic Kodak,

engineered so that the user could open a slot in the back and pencil onto each picture a caption like the ones used on the following pages. (For this, Eastman had paid the inventor $300,000—the largest sum paid by any industrial concern for a patent up to that time.)

One result of the boom in the new art of photography was an informal gallery of strong, confident American faces, in which a look of unmistakable serenity was preserved despite the doubts that were beginning to roil the nation. For the second decade was still in many ways a formal time when the broad middle layer of society remained carefully structured. And people tended to pose for the camera with the same formality they used in observing the patterned conventions of their lives—Sunday afternoon naps, orderly parades to church, family gatherings.

The names of the people in these photographs have receded with time. But in their studied attitudes, they represent an instantly recognizable record of the universal moments—weddings, birthdays, baptisms, outings—that knit together the middle-class backbone of America. The proud grandparent, the cherubic baby, the prideful farmer in his tall stand of corn—each carries in his eyes and in the posture of his body the signature of this time.

A pair of natty freelance photographers arrive in town with their equipment.

Second anniversary

First baby picture

Visiting with Grandma and Grandpa

Sunday at the stables

The girl next door

All dressed for the camping party

A day at the circus

Down in the old cornfield

Morning of the wedding

Fun and Games

Girl power wins again as a young charmer enlists two boys for rope skipping.

Defenders of the Faith of Childhood

Toys will fasten great truths in the memories of children which otherwise would be more difficult to impress on them.

SERMON BY A CHICAGO MINISTER

In their play, children create with the equipment they have at hand the world as they see it.

BUREAU OF EDUCATIONAL EXPERIMENTS, 1917

A bad moment for childhood came in 1917, when Christmas—or at least the exchange of Christmas gifts—was almost abolished by federal edict. After America intervened in the European conflict, the powerful Council of National Defense decided that an embargo on gifts would save materials for the war effort and would serve as a healthy reminder of the need for sacrifice at a time of crisis. At the last moment, a group of toy manufacturers galloped to the rescue and convinced the pragmatic Council that such gifts as air rifles and model cannons were responsible for making American boys the best soldiers in the world.

It was a close call, worthy of the fictional adventures of the Rover Boys or Tom Swift, which already had kids gnawing their fingernails to the quick. Even the piercing mind of Tom Swift (inventor of a diamond-making machine and an electric rifle in two 1911 novels) could hardly have devised a more telling argument than the one that the toy manufacturers used—that the play of children was not mere frivolity, but a vital learning process.

Along with the toy makers, who perhaps had their own best interests at heart, educators had begun to speak of children as diminutive philosophers, eagerly training themselves to cope with a bewildering world. John Dewey deplored parents who "look with impatience upon immaturity, regarding it as something to be got over as rapidly as possible"; the pioneering Italian teacher Maria Montessori took a swipe at the old notion of kids as lovable barbarians with the observation that "humanity shows itself in all its intellectual splendor during this tender age." Newspaper comics reflected this new attitude by viewing the world from the vantage point of the kids themselves. Such children's books as *Penrod* and Clara W. Hunt's *About Harriet* rejected the traditional fare of fantasy or adult adventure, and instead sympathetically explored the full range of the feelings of youngsters. Almost any adult could understand and even accept the spectacle of 12-year-old Penrod smoking a hayseed cigarette in his hideaway.

Such tolerance was certainly welcome, but to children, good fortune was perhaps most accurately measured by the repletion of their toy chests. In 1912, two-thirds of toy sales had come at Christmas, and many stores carried no toys during the rest of the year. By the end of the decade sales had almost tripled and the bounty of playthings—sampled at right and on the following pages, together with tempting descriptions from the original sales catalogues—raised the toy-chest level all year round.

Remarkably good at envisioning themselves in the driver's seat, kids had a field day with the transportation toys of the decade. Old-fashioned models that evoked travel by horse or bicycle were still popular. But the playthings that reflected the new technologies—airplanes, dirigibles and automobiles—had children making more noise and traveling faster in their imaginations than ever before.

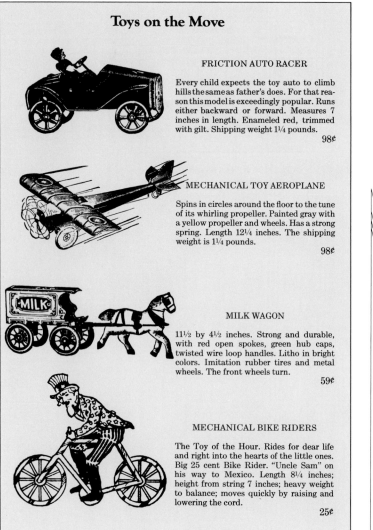

Toys on the Move

FRICTION AUTO RACER

Every child expects the toy auto to climb hills the same as father's does. For that reason this model is exceedingly popular. Runs either backward or forward. Measures 7 inches in length. Enameled red, trimmed with gilt. Shipping weight 1¼ pounds.

98¢

MECHANICAL TOY AEROPLANE

Spins in circles around the floor to the tune of its whirling propeller. Painted gray with a yellow propeller and wheels. Has a strong spring. Length 12¼ inches. The shipping weight is 1¼ pounds.

98¢

MILK WAGON

11½ by 4½ inches. Strong and durable, with red open spokes, green hub caps, twisted wire loop handles. Litho in bright colors. Imitation rubber tires and metal wheels. The front wheels turn.

59¢

MECHANICAL BIKE RIDERS

The Toy of the Hour. Rides for dear life and right into the hearts of the little ones. Big 25 cent Bike Rider. "Uncle Sam" on his way to Mexico. Length 8¼ inches; height from string 7 inches; heavy weight to balance; moves quickly by raising and lowering the cord.

25¢

Imaginary strains of the calliope sounded in children's rooms when the Humpty Dumpty Circus came to town—to stay—on Christmas Day. This miniature extravaganza was one of the most popular toys of the decade, partly because each of the figures in the circus was jointed so that it could be arranged in different positions, offering play possibilities that consumed countless blissful afternoons.

Circus Characters

Figures of wood, handsomely enameled in natural colors. Heads and limbs movable so figures can be set in variety of positions. Joints made with heavy rubber cord like French dolls, but much stronger. Elephants, 8 inches long; donkeys, 9 inches; clowns, 8 inches; chairs, 5 inches; ladders, 12 inches; stools or pedestals for animals, 2¾ inches. Our Best Outfit. Consists of 19 pieces.

$4.98

Fun and Games

Many a boy winced inwardly on Christmas or birthday when a well-intentioned aunt gave him an impenetrable biography of some great man. But it was a very different feeling to open up a package and discover a Mysto Magic Set, which instantly transformed him into Houdini; or an Erector Set, which enabled him to construct spectacular edifices—often resembling the Leaning Tower of Pisa.

Toys for Building Skills

CIRCULAR ALPHABET BOARD

An instructive toy. Made of metal and fibre. Diameter 12 inches. It has 80 letters and characters. Drawing slate in center. Shipping weight, 1½ pounds.

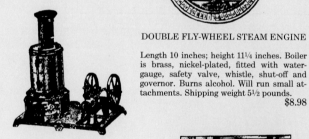

$1.39

DOUBLE FLY-WHEEL STEAM ENGINE

Length 10 inches; height 11¼ inches. Boiler is brass, nickel-plated, fitted with water-gauge, safety valve, whistle, shut-off and governor. Burns alcohol. Will run small attachments. Shipping weight 5½ pounds.

$8.98

HIGH GRADE PIANO

Made of good quality lumber in imitation mahogany finish. Nicely lithographed front. The little girl will be delighted with the exceptionally sweet tone of this piano. Has 15 keys. Length 15¾ inches; height 11 inches. Shipping weight 5 pounds.

$2.98

TELEGRAPH SET

Get that message! Sends and receives messages just as they do in real telegraph stations. Set consists of two actual working instruments, size of each 3½ x 2⅛ inches, and 10 feet of wire. Will carry ¼ mile. Morse code chart included. One dry cell works it. Shipping weight 1¼ pounds.

$1.19

"A well conducted toy shop is a fine kindergarten," wrote a toy maker. But youthful window-shoppers like this one probably never saw toys as anything but toys.

A Cure for Classroom Doldrums

In the eyes of his peers, it was a gullible child indeed who believed the claim of teachers that "learning can be fun." Grownups tended to swallow this idea, hook, line and sinker—especially if they read the 1912 best-selling book by the Italian educator Maria Montessori. Working with slum children in Italy, Dr. Montessori had devised a system of nursery and grade-school education, based on the use of playthings. Proselytizing magazine articles—such as the one excerpted below, from *McCall's Magazine*, April 1912—spread her ideas to every corner of America. To most kids, however, school still added up to a daily abridgment of freedom between the 8:05 and 3:30 bells.

For little boys and girls who love to play, there is now a new fairyland; a fairyland where there are no compulsory or disagreeable lessons to be learned, no books to be studied, no heavy tasks to do. In this strange country there is nothing to do but play. Wonderful toys have taken the place of study. Here little boys and girls learn reading, writing and arithmetic by playing marvelously engrossing games. True, in this remarkable garden for children there are schools—little boys and girls are doomed never to quite escape schools—there are wonderful schools and teachers, too. But wonder of wonders—teachers who do not teach and schools without lessons or books or desks!

The fairy godmother of this magic country is Maria Montessori. She dreamt of the wonders that should come to pass when all little boys and girls could live in the wonderful land of Study-by-Play. The result was the Montessori Childhood Educational method, based upon the Montessori didactic apparatus. This apparatus is made up of a large number of educational toys. These are toys that little boys and girls cannot even look at without learning something of color or proportion; toys that when played with teach little minds something of how to take care of the things that belong to them.

A clear idea of how this method is applied may best be gained by an examination of the educational apparatus used. The simplest games are those used in the development of the sense of touch. The child begins with little boards upon which are pasted alternate strips of rough and smooth papers. Large letters and numbers cut from both rough and smooth papers are pasted on cards. The child uses these letters first simply in distinguishing the smooth letters from the sandpaper ones. The little mind does not realize that these are the symbols that are to be later used in reading and writing and arithmetic. Much of the Montessori work is like this. The children become familiar with many fundamental forms long before they know what they are, or to what more advanced purposes they are to be put. This is the basis of the wonder of sense training. Every step is simplified by the foundation that has been laid. The child uses all its faculties and "sees with the fingers" as well as with the eyes.

Just here, we should look at another part of the educational apparatus used in training little fingers. Maria Montessori has invented a series of little frames by the use of which the child can simulate every act of dressing. On each of these frames, strips of cloth are mounted to be fastened together in various ways. There are frames to be fastened with ordinary buttons such as are found on children's coats and underwear. Then there are leather frames to be laced just as shoes are laced, and another one with buttonholes and shoe buttons to be fastened with a buttonhook just as the tiny shoes are fastened. Once a child has mastered these frames, no mere grown-up may ever again assist the child in dressing, for there is far too much pride in the new accomplishment to admit of assistance in its practical application.

Acrobatic Chicago girls, nattily attired in their Sunday hats, scramble aboard a makeshift seesaw, constructed by the kids of the neighborhood with leftover lumber.

167

Poised before the plunge, a gang of sledders with a speedy Flexible Flyer in the forefront, prepares to conquer the crusty snow on a hill in Cooperstown, New York.

The world closes in with awful swiftness upon a youngster, who faces the consequences of having miscalculated his position in the pecking order of the neighborhood.

Despite the efforts of adults to maintain a spirit of moral uplift among kids, violent impulses still tended to well up. Marjorie Jones, the girl friend of Booth Tarkington's hero, Penrod, learned this to her sorrow when she tauntingly called him a "little gentleman" just prior to the excerpt below. Unfortunately, she and her little brother happened to be standing beside a cauldron of tar at the time.

The big stone descended into the precise midst of the tar caldron and Penrod got his mighty splash. It was far, far beyond his expectations. A black sheet of eccentric shape rose out of the caldron and descended upon the three children, who had no time to evade it. When Marjorie and Mitchy-Mitch got their breath, they used it vocally; and seldom have more penetrating sounds issued from human throats. Coincidentally, Marjorie, quite berserk, laid hands upon the largest stick within reach and fell upon Penrod with blind fury. Attracted by the riot, Samuel Williams made his appearance, vaulting a fence, and was immediately followed by Maurice Levy and Georgie Bassett. "Penrod Schofield!" exclaimed Georgie Basset. "What does this mean?"

Marjorie leaned, panting, upon her stick. "I cu-called—uh—him—oh!" she sobbed—"I called him a lul—little—oh—gentleman! And oh—lu-look!—oh! lu-look at my du-dress!" Seizing the indistinguishable hand of Mitchy-Mitch, she ran wailing homeward down the street.

"Anybody has a perfect right," said Georgie, with dignity, "to call a person a little gentleman."

"You better look out!" Penrod was about to run amuck.

"I haven't called you a little gentleman, yet," said Georgie. "I only said it. Anybody's got a right to say it."

Bellowing, Penrod plunged his hand into the caldron, rushed upon Georgie and made awful work of his hair and features.

171

Real Kids on the Comic Page

Until the work of cartoonist Clare Briggs appeared in the comic sections of newspapers, the public image of children received pretty shabby treatment at the hands of funny-paper artists. The antic pranks and slipped-on-a-banana-peel violence of such cartoon characters as the Katzenjammer Kids and Buster Brown produced many belly laughs, but little genuine empathy. Clare Briggs wrought a remarkable softening of mood.

Originally a sketch artist for the press, Briggs turned to comics when his job was made obsolete by the increasing use of photographs in newspapers. To his new profession Briggs brought his great sketch-pad skill at catching details of expression with swift strokes of the pen. Evoking his own memories of growing up in a small village in Wisconsin (where he was nicknamed "Skin-nay," just like one of the characters in his comic serial, *The Days of Real Sport*), he specialized in the little incidents of childhood—the loss of a penny or the embarrassment of having to kiss a girl. Soon he had millions of readers smiling gently at the foibles of human nature in its formative stages. For each of Briggs's tiny cartoon dramas, selected on the following pages, journalist Wilbur D. Nesbit wrote a verse accompaniment that re-created both the sentimentality of America and the dialect of boyhood.

JUST
OUTDOORS

Indoors you can't do very much for fear you make a muss,
Outdoors is made for boys an' girls, an' good for all of us.
My pa he likes th' outdoors, too; he says th' Lord made *that*
An' mixed it up with hills an' trees, an' hummocky an' flat
So that it would be nice for folks and didn't skimp a bit—
Pa says th' Lord likes all outdoors—he made so much of it.

RECESS
AND
"CRACK THE WHIP"

Th' Willis boy that's just moved her
    —he's hardly ever played
A single game that us boys knows;
    he acts like he's afraid!
We learned him "crack th' whip"
    at recess time—him on th' end,
An' all of us whirled 'round an' 'rou
    an' then we let him bend!
Th' Willis boy knows *one* game now
    an' in a week, I'll bet
We'll have him 'nitiated
    in some more he won't forget!

THE
LOST
PENNY

Uncle Joseph he give me a cent,
An' it fell out sudden when I went
To'rds th' store—
    went right down through a crack;
Freckles Green,
    he jest won't give it back.
He crawled under for it,
    then sez: "Pshaw!
Findin's keepin's—Yes sir!
    That's th' law."

174

THE
DRIZZLY
DAY

[Y]ou can't go out, and you can't play
[W]henever it's a drizzly day.
[Y]ou got to set right in th' house
[An]d keep as still as any mouse.
[An]' your ma sez: "My goodness me!
[W]hy ain't you happy I can't see.
[Th]ere's lots of boys
[   ] would think it fine
[T]o have a home like yours and mine."

HOUSECLEANING
TIME

Housecleanin' time is fun alive!
We whoop around an' duck an' dive
Through where th' carpet's on th' line
—Play it's a tunnel—an' that's fine.
An' pa he come an' give a whack
Right through th' carpet on my back,
Then laughed:
    "I didn't know you's there."
But then I guess I didn't care.

POST
OFFICE

At Emmy Jones's birthday party
Buck Engledorf swelled up—the smarty!—
Buhcause Pearl Mulson called his name
In that tomfool post office game.
Huh! Buck ain't such a nawful wonder
That all of us must stand from under!
I guess he'd better get a girl—
I was the one that called out Pearl.

Playing a favorite American game with the biggest toy of all, kids of Lindstrom, Minnesota, wave an instant hello and goodby to a thundering express train.

The Great Outdoors

A determined hunter leads his wife along a ridge in Idaho.

The Call of the Wild

How much I always have desired and always shall desire to see Americans love their own splendid out-of-doors, and use it fairly and decently, like men and gentlemen!

EMERSON HOUGH IN *SUNSET, THE PACIFIC MONTHLY,* 1918

Americans had always been a vigorous, adventurous people, fiercely proud of their freedom to roam their continent and to hunt and to fish, whether for food or just for fun. But during the second decade the old American habit of being in the great outdoors became known as "recreation," a self-improving project to be pursued rather like a religion. Automobiles and increased leisure permitted so many tourists to hit the trail that the government feared they might kill all the wildlife and destroy the forests. Congress was impelled to set up a National Park Service in 1916 and impose rigid new limits on hunting.

So avid were America's new legions of outdoorsmen that in 1917, a war year, four New York counties reported 10,000 hunters had bagged 1,755 deer and 53 bears. By 1920 states had granted more than four million licenses to hunters, and the woods of Pennsylvania were so crowded with sportsmen firing wildly at anything moving that Lieutenant T. McKean Downs, a former artillery spotter with the American Expeditionary Force, swore he "felt safer in no-man's land during the battle of the Marne."

Moralistic in everything, Americans now managed to pontificate about the spiritual and mundane benefits of recreation. Magazines like *Outing* bristled with articles bearing titles like "The School of the Wilderness: What a Man Learns from his Neighbors, the Woods, the Waters and the Weather." *Sunset* magazine urged its readers to use their cars to get to vacation lands, but once there, to get out of their automobiles, since excessive driving led to "indigestion, blood pressure, brain fag and fatty degeneration." Another magazine, *The Survey,* asked the question "Is recreation statesmanlike?" and solemnly concluded that "recreation changes leisure hours from liabilities to assets."

Perhaps the most characteristic—and also ridiculous—preachment came from a hearty recreation director in California who extolled outdoor sport as the major influence on world history. Greece had surrendered to Rome, he maintained, because the Greeks had forgottten their games and turned to "painted women." Rome had also fallen when its men stopped roaming the woods and fields. Wrapping up the whole subject, the author calmly informed his public, "It looks as if the law of nations, which says that the Star of Empire shall rest upon that nation that plays long, hard and well, will hold true in California, and that in the future upon these Pacific shores will rise up the people who are destined to rule the world."

A huntress in Idaho poses proudly with her kill of pheasants. Ring-necks were not native to the U.S. but had been successfully imported and bred by hunters.

Spoofing their own hunting exploits, two Idaho girls, shotguns in hand, suspend their total day's bag (one squirrel) from a log big enough to hold a moose.

A trapper shows off a bearskin and the trap that got it for him. Though selling bearskins was legal, in 1918 Congress forbade the sale of such other game as waterfowl.

Making a genteel invasion of the great outdoors in their touring car, two bonneted ladies sit down with their husbands to a perfectly laid tentside breakfast table.

Famished after a morning of hunting, a country girl and her companions munch pie, while their fashionably attired horse peers out the cabin door.

Kneading bread at a roadside camp, a woman prepares dinner. Though roadside cabins were beginning to spring up, most people still preferred roughing it.

In the summer of 1917, many an American like the man above forgot the war for a moment and settled down to the ancient, peaceable business of angling.

Winter Fun

Revelers in bright costume watch skaters at the St. Paul, Minnesota, winter carnival.

Hot Time in the Cold Country

Blood, long sluggish in almost atrophied veins, began to flow again and in its rush from limb to limb gave new life and fresh strength to thousands who had almost forgotten the true meaning of outdoor sport.

BROCHURE FOR ST. PAUL OUTDOOR SPORTS CARNIVAL, 1916

For the greater part of their history, most Americans over the age of 12 or so had despised cold weather and looked upon snow as something either to be shoveled or simply endured. But in the second decade, as part of the new pursuit of leisure, surprising numbers of people shucked off old habits of hibernation and headed outside for a frolic at the first sprinkling of white. They celebrated the season not only with traditional sleds and skates, but with such newly-adopted sports as skiing and tobogganing, and most particularly with an American adaptation of an old European custom, the winter festival.

In 1911 Dartmouth College in Hanover, New Hampshire, held the first collegiate ice festival in the U.S. In 1916 and again in 1917, St. Paul, Minnesota, whose midwinter temperatures sometimes dropped to 40° below, held the biggest snow carnivals of all: the entire city of 200,000 turned out to prove that, despite blizzard and frostbite, an old-fashioned winter could be fun.

The festivities at these first annual St. Paul Outdoor Sports Carnivals, shown on these pages, began with whooping, bustling, foot-stomping parades. Dressed to the teeth in their warmest woollies, thousands of marchers trekked through the snow to salute a prominent citizen who had been designated Boreas Rex, the King of the North Wind. Every business and social club in town turned out for the show, each in a different costume, from the prison-like stripes of the Minnehaha Dry Cleaning Company and the Great Northern Railway's Glacier Park Marching Club *(opposite and overleaf)*, to the Indian get-up of the Weequah Canoe Club. Even the Salvation Army got into the act, exchanging its somber blue for outfits of a devilish red, duly inscribed "Be Saved Now."

But that was just for openers. In the middle of various streets around town the city fathers had set up a dozen man-made snow slides, ranging from a 95-foot-high ski jump for nervy athletes to gentler inclines for amateur tobogganers. On a nearby lake, frozen solid, crowds gathered to watch fancy skating and harness racing on the ice, and to marvel at motorized sleds that sped by at a breath-taking 65 miles an hour. And of course, as in any American festival worthy of the name, there were beauty queens—110 of them. Everybody loved it, and for one brief moment all manner of major calamities, from the war in Europe to the establishment of a U.S. income tax, faded away as the local newspapers boasted to their readers that "the eyes of the entire world are upon St. Paul."

SKATERS PIROUETTE IN AN ICE-DANCE.

There was no premium on sporting talent among the participants in St. Paul's winter carnival. Any kid with a toboggan could head for one of the dozen or so snowslides set up for the public in the city streets, while somebody out for a little more bounce had only to wait for an obliging marching club to come by with its blanket squad.

TOBOGGANERS ZIP DOWN A MAN-MADE SLOPE.

BLANKET HANDLERS GIVE A POISED TEAMMATE THE HEAVE-HO.

While Glacier Park's zestful sportsmen dominated
such events as push-ball, the big winners in
the carnival were the candidates for beauty queen.
When the time came for the 1916 coronation, Boreas
Rex demurred from making a choice and
proclaimed all 110 girls Queens of the North.

PLAYERS SCRAMBLE TO CONTROL AN OVERSIZED PUSH-BALL.

199

MINNEHAHA DRY CLEANERS *(LEFT)* AND GLACIER PARK EMPLOYEES TEAM UP IN A TUG-OF-WAR.

*Fastest action at the
carnival was provided by the motorized
sled racers (below), who roared
along at more than a
mile a minute, and by the tightly
bundled crews of the bucking,
plunging six-man toboggans
(right). But by all odds
the gamest of the winter sportsmen
in the carnival were the hardy
mushers who braved prairie
blizzards to drive their
dog teams 522 miles in a marathon
all the way from Winnipeg,
Manitoba, to St. Paul.*

MOTOR-SLED RIDERS GIVE A STARTING WAVE.

202

A TOBOGGAN TEAM HURTLES PAST A LARGE, VERY SOLID TREE.

HIS JOVIAL MAJESTY, BOREAS REX, LEADS HIS ENTOURAGE THROUGH THE SNOW.

205

The War

New York's 69th Infantry bids the girls goodbye.

The Yanks Take On Kaiser Bill

Good-bye, Maw! Good-bye, Paw!

Good-bye, Mule, with yer old hee-haw!

I'll git you a Turk an' a Kaiser too—

An' that's about all one feller can do!

"LONG BOY"—A WORLD WAR I BALLAD

With great reluctance—but firm purpose—President Woodrow Wilson called for a declaration of war against Germany on April 2, 1917. In so doing he assured the nation and the world that "We have no selfish ends to serve. We desire no conquest, no dominion. We seek no indemnities . . . no material compensation."

Every red-blooded American male was prepared to leap into the breach and every woman and child to back up the doughboys. But no one quite knew what to do. The United States had not fought a major war in over 50 years. The Army had a grand total of 208,034 men. The air service counted 55 rickety planes and 130 pilots.

The lack of manpower, if not of expertise, was quickly remedied by the draft. But as Theodore Roosevelt wrote, "the enormous majority of our men in the encampments were drilling with broomsticks or else with rudely whittled guns. . . . In the camps I saw barrels mounted on sticks on which zealous captains were endeavoring to teach their men how to ride a horse."

Civilians began organizing war-bond rallies, saving peach pits for gas masks and hunting down real or imagined German spies. Advertisers embraced the patriotic theme; one cigar manufacturer pictured a wise smoker confiding: "I do not fancy pacifist cigars that weakly proffer peace. Nor do I like barbaric autocrats who war upon my day's efficiency. In Robert Burns I found the mildly militant cigar I thought did not exist."

So wholly unprepared was the United States at the onset of war that the British and French had to sell American troops most of their artillery, tanks and ammunition. Not until June 1918 did American industry get into full production for the business of war. Factories were reorganized to work around the clock. Food dealers diverted tons of groceries to the men in the trenches.

The result of the nation's colossal efforts, as everyone had expected, was a glorious victory. And a relatively painless one, too; in contrast to the millions of European fatalities, only 116,516 American soldiers and sailors died during the conflict—and more than half died from disease. American business had boomed during the war years, and the United States had become the most powerful country in the world economically, and perhaps militarily too. So splendidly had everyone struggled at home and abroad that the whole nation had to agree that the United States had achieved the goal originally set by President Wilson: "The world must be made safe for democracy."

Learning to knit woollies for the boys "over there," a patriotic fireman in Michigan takes up needles and yarn under the guidance of a skilled neighbor lady.

Raw recruits, still slouching in their civvies, get a demonstration salute from their new sergeant at a National Guard camp in New York's Van Cortlandt Park.

" You're in the Army Now "

On June 5, 1917, between 7 a.m. and 7 p.m. nearly 10 million men, filled with patriotic fervor and heroic notions, went to their local voting places to register for the draft. But when the boys—all straw hats and awkwardness—actually arrived in camp, their initial ardor to "kill the Kaiser" quickly changed to bewilderment. For a civilian army predominantly composed of small-town boys and farmers, Army life was as foreign as the enemy they longed to fight. The food was awful, voluntary classes in French were utterly mystifying. The four daily hours of drill seemed only vaguely related to the conquest of the Hun, and paralyzing lectures on "personal hygiene and care of the feet" were lacking in heroic glamor. The reflections of soldiers on the Army were satirized *(overleaf)* by serviceman Edward Streeter in *"Dere Mable,"* a collection of imaginary letters written by a rookie to his sweetheart.

Dere Mable:

I got some news for you, Mable. The cook says we only drew ten days supply of food last time. He says he guesses when we et that up well go to France. Hes an awful smart fello the cook. Hes got a bet on that if the allys dont buck up an win the Germans is comin out ahead. Were all eatin as fast as we can. Perhaps we can eat it all in less than ten days. So maybe well be gone, Mable, before I rite you from here again.

Theres a French sargent comes round once in a while an says the war is goin to be over quick. He ought to know cause hes been over there an seen the whole thing. He smokes cigarets something awful an dont say much. Thats because the poor cus cant talk much English. It must be awful not to talk English. Think of not bein able to say nothing all your life without wavin your arms round an then lookin it up in a dickshunary.

I feel so sorry for these fellos that Im studiin French a lot harder sos theyll have someone to talk to when we get over there. Im readin a book now thats rote all in French. No English in it anywhere, Mable. A fello told me that was the only way to talk it good. I dont understand it very well so far. The only way I kno its French is by the picturs. Some day Im goin to find out what the name is. Then Im goin to get the English of it. Those are some picturs. Aint I fierce, Mable? I guess thats why I get on with wimen so well.

I gave up readin it out loud cause the fellos said it made em think they was in Paris so much they got restles. I cant speak no better yet. I guess that comes at the end of the book.

As soon as we got the hot shouers all fixed the pipes busted. So the other day the Captin walked us all in town to take a bath. I didnt need one much. I used my head more than most of em. Last fall when it was warm I took as many as two a week an got away ahead of the game. I went along though. More for the walk than anything.

I saw the Captin didnt make no move to take a bath hisself. I

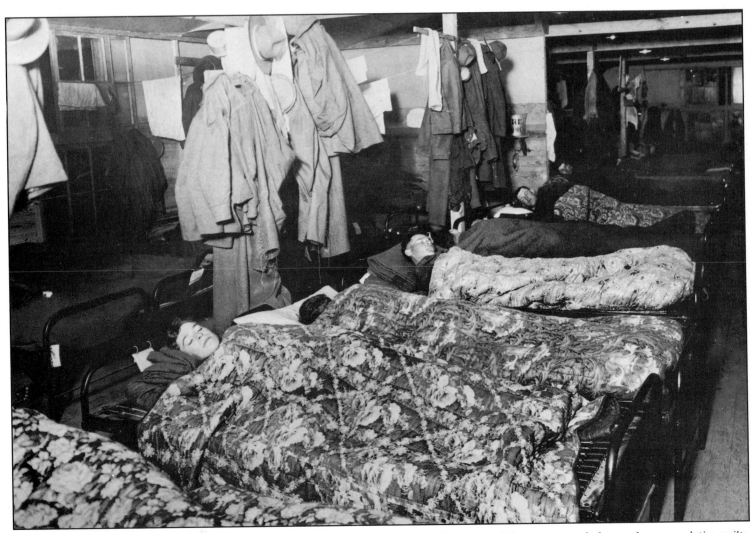

Rookies turn in at 10 p.m. on Long Island. Their quarters were not yet finished; they had to hang their clothes on pegs and sleep under nonregulation quilts.

thought he might be shy. He dont mix very well with the fellos. I felt sorry for him. Everyone else was laffin and throwin things with him standin off an noone throwin a thing at him. I went up and says "Aint you goin to take a bath this winter to, Captin?" Just jolly, Mable, that all. I says, "You dont want to mind the bunch. They dont care a bit. There as dirty as you are anyway. Probably more." An I bet they were Mable cause I aint seen the Captin do a stroke of work since we come here. Just stands round givin orders.

I says, "If noone wont lend you a towel you can use mine. I was just goin to have it washed anyway." I thought he was goin to choke. Hes awful queer.

Just like the other mornin he calls me over an says, "Smith, my orderlies sick. You can shine my boots this mornin." He said it like Id been beggin him to for a month. An then he says "Smith you can lite the fire in my stove." He had me thinkin he was doin me favors. He said I might put some oil on his boots if

I wished. I says that would be a great treat an I wished he wouldnt be so kind or the fellos would think he was playin favorites. I guess he didnt here me Mable cause hed just gone out. I said it anyway. I didnt care if he wasnt there. Spunky. Thats me all over.

I couldnt find no oil for his boots anywhere, Mable, so I poured some out of his lamp. An then I dont think that suited him. Queer fello the Captin.

Im ritin this in the Y.M.C.A. in the afternoon cause Im goin on guard tonite. I dont see why they dont make it a permenant detail and be done with it. Someone said the top sargents a man of one idea. I guess Im the idea. I didnt go out to drill this afternoon. I didnt say nothin to the sargent though cause sargents have an idea that if they dont get a lot of fellos to go out to drill with them they dont look popular. I got to go now sos to get in my tent before they come from drill.

As ever
on guard, Bill

Officers at Camp Custer, Michigan, attend a lesson in French, to prepare for "gay Paree." Besides such classes, mess tables were set aside for French conversation.

Mrs. William Randolph Hearst (in flowered hat), wife of America's most powerful newspaper publisher, reviews a Liberty Loan parade on New York's East Side.

MUST CHILDREN DIE AND MOTHERS PLEAD IN VAIN ?

Buy More
LIBERTY BONDS

Dollars for Democracy

As an aid in financing the war, the government launched four drives to sell "Liberty bonds." Celebrities by the hundreds appealed to audiences to buy bonds; President Wilson himself appeared at a Broadway show, asking theatergoers to subscribe. Volunteer salesmen took the campaign to neighborhoods across the country, and the smallest children filled Liberty Books with 25-cent stamps ("Lick a Stamp and Lick the Kaiser").

The most dramatic of the bond rallies were staged in Manhattan, in front of the U.S. Sub-Treasury Building *(overleaf)* and at the New York Public Library on Fifth Avenue. In one bond-peddling skit, movie idol Douglas Fairbanks wore boxing gloves labeled "Victory" and "Liberty Bonds." Predictably, he knocked out the Kaiser. The result of such razzle-dazzle: bond drives were oversubscribed and the government netted almost $17 billion.

Under the paternal hand of George Washington, megaphone-wielding Douglas Fairbanks warms up a throng of prospective bond buyers during a Wall Street rally.

Although born in Austria-Hungary, opera singer Ernestine Schumann-Heinck, escorted by two doughboys, comes on as 100 per cent American at a bond rally.

Women in Newark, New Jersey, learn to repair an automobile. One woman writer of the day feared such training would unsuit girls for "American family life."

The Women Take Over

As more and more men were drafted into the Army, women stepped forward to fill the jobs the boys had left behind. Suddenly, a male-dominated America was confronted with the spectacle of women auto mechanics, telegraph messengers, elevator operators and streetcar conductors —and that was not all. They toiled on factory assembly lines, carried ice, plowed fields and became traffic cops. Women invaded even the sanctuary of the armed forces, about 11,000 female yeomen enlisting in the Navy as clerks and stenographers.

Committees for the protection of girls worried about the effect on female morals. But the girls themselves found their work uplifting, as shown *(overleaf)* in a condensation from an article entitled "Wartime, the Place and the Girl," written for *The Independent* magazine by one Norma B. Kastl, an interviewer in a service bureau for lady workers.

219

The Government gas mask factory has proved a most interesting field for many artists, musicians and stage women. One well-known portrait painter is now spending her days in turning over little brass disks and carefully inspecting both sides. Another woman who has created several famous character parts on Broadway gets up every morning at half past five and takes the early train into New York to get to the factory at eight o'clock. During the recent speeding-up period, caused by urgent calls from our armies overseas, she reached home often as late as ten or eleven at night. But did she mind? Not she! "I would not have missed it for anything," she said. "It has been one of the richest experiences of my life—meeting all the wonderful women who are there, not only the professional women but the little seam-stresses and factory girls who have given up their old work to do their bit—and all the time feeling that I was being really useful to the boys on the other side."

The navy is taking on women as yeomen to do shore duty at the wireless stations. Being a yeoman is not so merely picturesque as the newspapers would have us believe. To be sure you can wear a uniform, but you also work seven days a week and enlist for the duration of the war. Definite war service it is, however, and every girl who becomes a yeoman can have the satisfaction of knowing that she is releasing, as from prison, some sailor who has been fuming with impatience and disappointment because he had to spend his days in an office instead of on the deck of a destroyer somewhere on the Atlantic.

Dressed for hard work, two girls hoist a chunk of ice. Some girls were paid male wages in keeping with the feminist slogan, "Equal Pay for Equal Work."

Mrs. Thomas Wasselle, age 22, paints a smokestack in Oakland, California. When her husband was drafted, she decided to take his place as a steeple jack.

FEED a FIGHTER
Eat only what you need —
Waste nothing —
That he and his family
may have enough

UNITED STATES FOOD ADMINISTRATION

Hooverizing to Beat the Hun

As the country girded for war, Food Administrator Herbert Hoover launched a national program of voluntary food rationing by instituting wheatless Mondays and Wednesdays, meatless Tuesdays and porkless Thursdays and Saturdays. In order to implement this belt-tightening program, which came to be called "Hooverizing," the Food Administrator urged families to plant backyard gardens. He also asked Americans to substitute such exotic viands as whale meat for beefsteak and to eat an awful, rough-grained substance known as Victory Bread.

In other spartan gestures, coal was conserved on heatless Mondays, and the manufacture of liquor was suspended—much to the delight of prohibitionists. Perhaps the grandest gesture of all came from motorists who observed gasless Sundays by hitching up the team to the front bumper before starting out on a patriotic auto trip.

A resourceful New York family takes a spin while faithfully conforming to the government's plea to all automobile owners to conserve gasoline on Sundays.

Keeping Fit for the Fight

Barely a month after America got into the war, virtually everyone was trying to find some way to rally behind the grand old flag. Paunchy businessmen, harking to the faint possibility of a genuine call to arms, subjected themselves to the "Daily Dozen" system of fitness exercises devised by Yale's great former football coach, Walter Camp. Women and children were just as earnest about preparing for their own wholly improbable call-up. Shrugging into baggy greatcoats and *bas couture* campaign hats, housewives marched off for afternoons of calisthenics, rifle practice and even extended-order drill. Before long, many an otherwise genteel matron knew how to rendezvous on the double and to shoot a Springfield or Krag rifle reasonably close to the target. And of course every kid in the country happily took his fling *(overleaf)* at the exciting neighborhood game of the 20th Century called Trench Warfare.

Ex-President William Howard Taft (right foreground, in suspenders) lines up for exercises with Walter Camp's Home Defense Guards in a Yale gymnasium.

Four of Uncle Sam's smaller doughboys make a wild leap over the top, their toy rifles raised for the assault on an imaginary trench full of cowering Germans.

On the range in Wakefield, Massachusetts, lady volunteers—most of them wives or mothers of men at the front—are shown how to hold rifles by U.S. Marines.

With a whoop and a giggle, members of the American Women's League for Self Defense launch a practice attack on the Hun at Governors Island, New York.

A Hand from the Home Folks

As the war effort got into gear, the home folks helped in many touching ways. They responded to Red Cross appeals by knitting quantities of woolens to keep the soldiers warm—notwithstanding the doubts of a skeptic named Samuel Dale, who wrote to the Brookline, Massachusetts, *Chronicle* that an Army major "told us he had never seen a soldier in active service wearing a sweater and had not been able to find a soldier who had ever seen a soldier in active service wearing a sweater." Housewives and kids saved tons of fruit pits, which were burned to make charcoal filters for gas masks. Families cleaned out their bookshelves to give the soldiers reading matter. But some of the gifts suggested that not all the donors acted from altruism; many of the gifts were unsuitable. Let's not have "a mere house-cleaning," scolded *The Literary Digest* on April 20, 1918; its article is excerpted on page 231.

At a grain warehouse turned into a canteen in Yonkers, New York, Red Cross ladies line up to hand out sandwiches and smiles to soldiers from a neighboring camp.

Standing on a mountain of already donated volumes, an amiable barker calls for still more books from passers-by outside the New York Public Library on Fifth Avenue.

In asking for books to send to the boys at the front those in charge of the work do not expect any valuable library to be despoiled in the eagerness of those at home to add to the pleasure and comfort of those "over there." But they think it would be just as well to use a little care and discretion in the selection, and not turn an act that ought to brim with thoughtful sympathy into a mere house-cleaning.

It is reasonably certain that those in the trenches do not care a hang how some professional woman preserves her beauty, how to do fancy needlework or even how women love. Nor have they much time to devote to the care and feeding of infants. Certainly the "Undertaker's Review" would seem to have a Hunnish sug-

gestiveness. And yet all these are being sent over—that is, they are being thoughtlessly contributed. Fortunately they do not reach the other side, for they are carefully weeded out, but it is extremely probable that those who make such careless contributions have more time to devote to selection than the busy men and women who are handling the tons of volumes being sent. Ruskin's "Letter to Young Girls," "Directions for Needlework," and "How Women Love" are coming in galore.

Another enlightening book that made its debut to the stacks yesterday was one entitled "Diseases of Dogs." Owing to the fact that General Pershing has tabued mascots, however, the Board of Book Censors will have to pass up the bow-wow stuff.

Ankle-deep in peach stones, three Chicago Red Cross ladies pack away. Seven pounds of pits made the filter for a single gas mask; a million men required masks.

Looking none the worse for their venture into woman's work, some well-scrubbed boys in Cooperstown, New York, take up needles to knit for trench-bound soldiers.

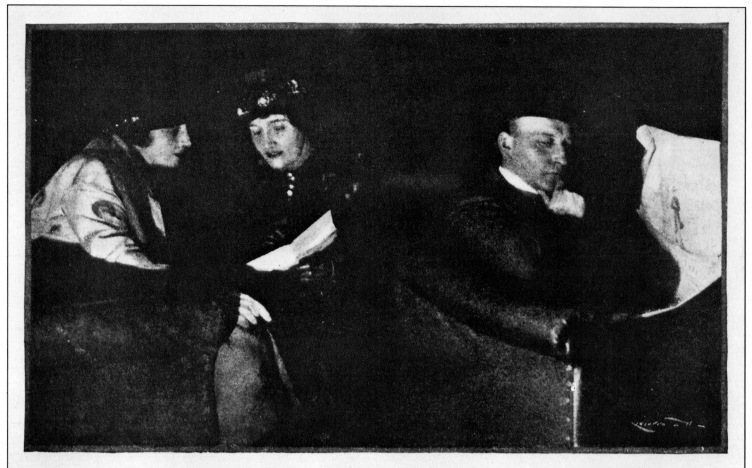

Spies and Lies

German agents are everywhere, eager to gather scraps of news about our men, our ships, our munitions. It is still possible to get such information through to Germany, where thousands of these fragments—often individually harmless —are patiently pieced together into a whole which spells death to American soldiers and danger to American homes.

But while the enemy is most industrious in trying to collect information, and his systems elaborate, he is *not* super-human—indeed he is often very stupid, and would fail to get what he wants were it not deliberately handed to him by the carelessness of loyal Americans.

Do not discuss in public, or with strangers, any news of troop and transport movements, or bits of gossip as to our military preparations, which come into your possession.

Do not permit your friends in service to tell you— or write you—"inside" facts about where they are, what they are doing and seeing.

Do not become a tool of the Hun by passing on the malicious, disheartening rumors which he so eagerly sows. Remember he asks no better service than to have you spread his lies of disasters to our soldiers and sailors, gross scandals in the Red Cross, cruelties, neglect and wholesale executions in our camps, drunkenness and vice in the Expeditionary Force, and other tales certain to disturb American patriots and to bring anxiety and grief to American parents.

And do not wait until you catch someone putting a bomb under a factory. Report the man who spreads pessimistic stories, divulges—or seeks—confidential military information, cries for peace, or belittles our efforts to win the war.

Send the names of such persons, even if they are in uniform, to the Department of Justice, Washington. Give all the details you can, with names of witnesses if possible— show the Hun that we can beat him at his own game of collecting scattered information and putting it to work. The fact that you made the report will not become public.

You are in contact with the enemy *today*, just as truly as if you faced him across No Man's Land. In your hands are two powerful weapons with which to meet him—discretion and vigilance. *Use them.*

COMMITTEE ON PUBLIC INFORMATION
8 JACKSON PLACE, WASHINGTON, D. C.

George Creel, Chairman
The Secretary of State
The Secretary of War
The Secretary of the Navy

The Great Witch Hunt

Before delivering his request for a declaration of war to Congress President Wilson had predicted: "Once lead this people into war, and they'll forget there was ever such a thing as tolerance; to fight you must be brutal and ruthless, and the spirit of ruthless brutality will enter into the very fibre of our national life, infecting Congress, the courts, the policeman, the man in the street."

The President was right. Once the excitement of marching in parades and cheering at bond rallies was overshadowed by the serious business of being in a shooting war, the mood of the nation underwent a violent, even vicious change. Dissent died away to a whisper and orthodoxy of expression and action was enforced. To question the nobility of the war effort was tantamount to treason.

This almost unanimous commitment to war amounted to an abrupt about-face for much of the nation. During the three years since Europe had erupted in total war, Americans had been far from total agreement as to what stand the country should take. Many people in the Northeast had favored all aid to the Allies short of intervention, while people farther west, where the physical distance from Europe was greater and the number of recent immigrants smaller, remained isolationists. A few militants, fired up by the likes of belligerent Teddy Roosevelt, had clamored for military "preparedness." But equal numbers of pacifists had agreed heartily with the isolationist stand of the New York *World:* "If Europe insists on committing suicide, Europe must furnish the corpse for Europe's funeral." One of the most popular songs of 1915 was "I Didn't Raise My Boy to Be a Soldier."

As the war grew fiercer in Europe, however, more and more Americans found themselves in sympathy with the Allies. This feeling developed into real outrage against the Germans when numbers of German spies were discovered sabotaging American industry and manipulating American opinion. On July 24, 1915, a U.S. Secret Service agent had managed to snatch a brief case from Dr. Heinrich Albert, the No. 1 German agent in the United States. The contents of the brief case, amplified by other evidence, revealed that Albert had received $28 million from the German government to finance a wide variety of disruptive acts. For example, German agents had placed a time bomb aboard a steamship carrying sugar from New York to France, had started fires and had created "accidents" in several U.S. munitions plants working for the Allies. Spies had also attempted to stir up strikes at the Bethlehem Steel Company. In order to woo the United States to the German side, Albert's men had arranged to produce pro-German films and had even bought a New York daily, *The Mail,* and filled it with propaganda.

When the United States actually entered the war, all German agents not arrested in the Albert roundup fled across the Mexican border. Nonetheless, overly zealous Americans continued to see spies—nearly all of them hallucinatory—in every country town, on every factory assembly line, lurking around every public reservoir. The government, fearing that saboteurs would bomb railroad bridges, stationed a soldier at either end of every major bridge; passengers on the rear platforms of trains were ushered into the club car whenever the train passed over a bridge, so that no one could toss out a bomb.

Wherever a whisper was planted, a full-grown rumor sprang up a moment later. One story had it that President Wilson's secretary, Joseph Tumulty, had been imprisoned as a German spy and shot. Tumulty himself had to proclaim publicly that he was innocent and very much alive. The rumors flew. Enemy agents on the Atlantic coast were flashing instructions to German U-boats. Horses waiting to be shipped to France had been infected with bacteria. Mexican bandits were being prompted to invade the United States. A headline in *The New York Times* shrieked: "Red Cross Bandages Poisoned by Spies." The federal government, far from calming the spy mania, nursed it along. A special propaganda agency, the Committee on Public Information, was set up by the President under a newspaperman named George Creel. Creel enlisted 75,000 "Four-Minute Men" to deliver brief patriotic speeches to crowds at movie houses and legitimate theaters all over the country. Artists like Charles Dana Gibson, creator of the elegant Gibson girl, and writers of the stature of Booth

Tarkington were commissioned to create posters like the one on page 234, along with cartoons, advertisements and syndicated features urging citizens to "'Stamp' Out the Kaiser" and ferret out spies.

The spy scare soon led to suspicion of anyone who seemed to retain some tie to a foreign country. Treason charges by the carload were hurled against the nation's more recent immigrants, particularly those who had come from countries governed by the Central Powers. German-Americans, Hungarian-Americans, Austrian-Americans, Jewish-Americans—all these national or religious groups were condemned under the new label, "hyphenated Americans," meaning Americans of divided loyalty.

Naturally, the German-Americans suffered the most bitter attacks. In 1917 more than two million Americans were of actual German birth, and millions more were of

German descent. Before the war, German-Americans had been regarded as ideal citizens, and many American racists had theorized about the innate superiority of the "Teutons." But now that the popular imagination summoned up the picture of treasonous German-Americans, critics like psychologist G. Stanley Hall, previously an admirer of everything Teutonic, announced that "there was something fundamentally wrong with the Teutonic soul."

Again, Washington abetted the hatemongers. Employers were asked to check into the national origins of workers and to guarantee their loyalty. As a result of these drumhead investigations, many Americans with German names were fired from their jobs. In some workshops men with foreign accents were forced to crawl across the floor and kiss the American flag. Others were accused of seditious statements and publicly flogged or tarred and

Minnesota children display signs identifying them as "100 per cent patriots." On the opposite page the press takes two widely differing views of super-Americanism.

feathered. At some war bond rallies, German-Americans were forced to parade as objects of ridicule. An angry mob in Omaha tried in vain to lynch a German-American youngster; a mob in southern Illinois succeeded.

Symphony conductors avoided works by Mozart and Beethoven. Dr. Karl Muck, the German conductor of the Boston Symphony, was fired and interned as a dangerous alien. States like Delaware, Iowa and Montana outlawed the teaching of courses in the German language and culture, and librarians across the country removed books by German authors from their shelves. Publishers of textbooks for schools tried to discredit rival firms by arguing that competitors were German sympathizers. One history book was attacked for simply publishing a picture of the Kaiser, another for showing Frederick the Great.

Hollywood got into the act by releasing a series of hate films: *To Hell with the Kaiser, Wolves of Kultur* and the most famous, *The Kaiser, The Beast of Berlin.* So provocative was *The Beast of Berlin* that patriotic societies in Omaha advertised it with signs on streetcars and a hanged effigy of "the Beast" himself. A typical hate movie showed mad German scientists training houseflies to carry germs into the United States on millions of tiny feet. One publicist of the day characterized the German in American movies as "the hideous Hun, a fiendish torturer and sadist who thought no more of raping a ten-year-old girl than of sweeping a priceless piece of Sèvres from the table to make room for his feet in the French chateau invariably commandeered as his headquarters."

Finally, in a burst of anti-German fervor, Americans changed the name of German measles to "liberty" measles, hamburger to "liberty steak," sauerkraut to "liberty

---

We have cherished and honored in this country during the last twenty years a type of mind totally different from any of the types to which our government owes its organization, our commercial system its development, our country its growth. It is the most destructive mind in the world, the most grasping and unabashed, one of the ablest, one of the most aspiring, and, in its own view, the most concerned for human welfare. It is the mind, one type of which was exhibited the other day in Kansas City at the trial of Mrs. Rose Pastor Stokes for violation of the Espionage Act. Mrs. Stokes is a Jewess, born in Russia. The Russian Jews of her sort—the intellectual sort—have no national feeling.

In Baruch and scores of like men we see it [the Jewish mind] working for the good of the country. But what of the Hearst Jews that Hearst is so tender of? What of the I.W.W. Jews, the revolutionary Russian Jews, of whom Hillquit is one, with all breeds of bats in their noisy belfries?

Mr. Wilson says the war is knitting us all together. These vari-ous and somewhat ominous Jewish brethren—what of them? As the knitting goes on shall they be a part of the yarn, or are the rest of us to be the yarn and they the needles?

EDITORIAL IN THE OLD HUMOR MAGAZINE *LIFE,* JUNE 20, 1918

With all our preparing, we must not overlook preparedness of soul. When so many indications point to our soon being in a state of war, we ought all to be casting about for every aid we can find in making ready to quit us like men. We must prepare to withstand the passions of the mob; to see to it that aliens among us are perfectly secure in property and life. We must see to it that freedom of conscience, of press, and of speech shall not be abrogated; that tolerance and respect for others shall rule us. We must prepare to brace ourselves against disappointments; to remain undismayed by the clamors of the press; to keep calm in the midst of tempests. All boasting and vengeful shouting are to be sternly avoided.

EDITORIAL IN THE *NEW YORK EVENING POST,* MARCH 24, 1917

cabbage," dachshunds to "liberty pups." In Cincinnati, pretzels were banned from lunch counters.

Teddy Roosevelt was behind a movement to convert all "hyphenated Americans" into "100 per cent Americans." He insisted that everyone subscribe to "the simple and loyal motto, AMERICA FOR AMERICANS," and roundly condemned "those who spiritually remain foreigners in whole or in part." To become "100 per cent American" it was not enough for a hyphenated American to support the government and obey the laws of his adopted land; he had to abandon all traces of the customs, beliefs and language he had brought with him from the Old Country. Bowing to such coercion, thousands renounced their heritage, joined patriotic clubs and attended public meetings where long, fervent loyalty addresses were delivered.

Henry Ford instituted among his foreign-born employees a compulsory English-language school where the first thing his students learned to say was "I am a good American." Later they participated in a pageant in which, dressed in national costume, they marched into a huge melting pot from which another line of men emerged wearing identical suits and waving little American flags.

Before long this insistence on conformity was applied to everyone and almost everything. Congress passed wartime laws against espionage and sedition that established heavy penalties for criticizing the government, the Constitution, the flag, the uniforms of the Army and Navy, any Allied nation, or for obstructing the sale of United States War Bonds. Under these laws an offender could be fined up to $10,000 and/or receive 20 years in prison for advocating a reduced production of war necessities or for saying anything "disloyal, profane, scurrilous, or abusive" about any aspect of the government or the war effort. A supplementary court decision forbade historians to disagree in any way with the official explanation of the causes of World War I, which held that Germany had been entirely at fault.

So zealously prosecuted were these laws, which clearly violated the spirit of the First Amendment, that about 6,000 people were arrested and 1,500 sentenced, many for simply criticizing the Red Cross or the YMCA. The producer of a film entitled *The Spirit of '76* served three years in prison for showing British soldiers killing American women and children during the American Revolution. Two leading Socialists, Eugene V. Debs and Mrs. Rose Stokes, were sentenced. Debs, convicted of speaking in violation of the Espionage Act, was still in prison in 1920 when he ran for President and won nearly a million votes. Mrs. Stokes received 10 years for writing a letter to a newspaper that read, "I am for the people, and the government is for the profiteers" (her conviction was later set aside). Labor leader Big Bill Haywood and 100 other leaders of the Industrial Workers of the World were sentenced to prison for advocating strikes among oppressed workers and for publishing allegedly antiwar propaganda. By the end of 1918, more than 1,000 I.W.W. members had been arrested and some 500 indicted.

The monumental efforts of the government and of private citizens stifled dissent in the United States to a degree that would have seemed impossible before the war. The Post Office forbade mailing privileges to all periodicals that did not completely echo the government's policies. The rest of the press accepted "voluntary" self-censorship of war news and criticism of the war. Every native American faced very heavy penalties for dissent, and every foreigner risked deportation. The chairman of the Iowa Council of Defense spoke for millions of his fellow citizens when he announced: "We are going to love every foreigner who really becomes an American, and all others we are going to ship back home."

Despite all this frantic witch-hunting, probably only a handful of those convicted were actually spies. As one federal judge declared a year after the war was over: "I assert as my best judgment that more than 90 percent of the reported pro-German plots never existed." His opinion was seconded by John Lord O'Brian, a high official in the Department of Justice, who asserted that "no other one cause contributed so much to the oppression of innocent men" as the nation's wartime hysteria over what was supposedly "an all-pervasive system of German espionage."

Burning books by German authors, citizens of Baraboo, Wisconsin, express the chauvinism of an aroused nation. Some zealots banned even scholarly texts by Germans.

The View from the City Desk

With the coming of war, the nation's press turned its energy to telling the country what was going on over there. Unknown to the general public, the accuracy of the written news that reached the States was spotty at best. A typical example was the Associated Press blood and thunder account *(condensed below)* of the "lost battalion"; the reports of the Germans' surrender demand, the American commander's brash reply and the whole cavalier aura of the story were pure nonsense. But in addition to colorfully embroidered war tales, newspapers of this decade also gave their readers something excitingly authentic and new in war coverage: photo-journalism presented in brown-tinted rotogravure sections, which were introduced to America by *The New York Times* in 1914. As re-created on the following pages, the Sunday "roto" brought home an intimate feeling for the war as it was really being fought.

With the American forces northwest of Verdun—The brightest spot in the heroic and amazing story of the now famous "lost battalion," as yet untold, was the climax to the fourth day of the siege in the Argonne Forest.

When the men had been for a long time without food and when many were weak from exhaustion, but not one despairing, an American who had been taken prisoner by the Germans suddenly appeared at the little camp surrounded by the valley. He had been sent blindfolded from the German headquarters with a note to Major Whittlesey, the battalion commander, reading:

"Americans, you are surrounded on all sides. Surrender in the name of humanity. You will be well treated."

Major Whittlesey did not hesitate a fraction of a second.

"Go to hell!" he shouted. His men, despite their weariness and hunger, and in imminent danger every moment, cheered so loudly that the Germans heard them from their observation posts.

The same spirit animating them to plunge ahead in the forest to their perilous position maintained them at that moment, and every man, wounded or well, enthusiastically approved Major Whittlesey's abrupt answer.

A composite story, gleaned from a dozen recitals, reveals that the battalion when ordered to advance last Friday, in the eagerness to catch up with the retreating Germans, gradually spread out and widened its ranks. This allowed the Germans to infiltrate unseen behind the Americans.

The enemy had planned to catch the Americans in a hollow surrounded on all four sides by heights, the greatest of which was a steep hill directly ahead. The Americans, filled with eagerness, dashed into this hollow without stopping to think that the enemy might be awaiting them. The battalion proceeded half way up the hill, then discovered that the Germans on both sides had jointly flanked them and had closed in on their rear.

Daily American aviators, searching vainly for the battalion, flew overhead, but no outcry the men could make brought anything but a volley of shouts and laughter from the Germans in front and behind and to the right and left of them. The beleaguered men discovered that there were German machine-gun nests all around them, every fifteen feet or so, and for a man to show himself was the signal for a sweeping rain of bullets.

As the days passed the Americans grew more and more emaciated, but they never gave up hope. There was nothing but a grim determination to hold out until the last man was finished.

Major Whittlesey had his entire battalion behind him to a man, and the correspondent was told that the men jeered at the idea of surrender, declaring that they never would have given up.

ASSOCIATED PRESS, OCTOBER 11, 1918.

MEN AT WAR

The doughboys get the job done on the Western Front.

No newsman's comment on the Great War was more vivid than that written across the face of this battle-weary infantry corporal in the Argonne Forest.

The Yanks arrive in France, leaping in pairs onto the docks at Brest.

When the doughboys stepped ashore, they fell in with a bustle of activity the like of which they had never seen: rickety French freig cars, renovated to carry "quarante hommes ou huite chevaux," armor tanks being shipped into battle, and rows of biplanes and leather-c

Taking a break during the march, infantrymen soak their feet in a ditch.

Getting ready for the Meuse-Argonne offensive in September 1918, soldiers fast

iators such as those of the 11th Aero Bombardment Squadron, above. r a while, the U.S. soldiers were swept up by the excitement of the ar- al scene. Before long, however, the reality of war closed in upon em as they trundled onto rail cars and trucks headed for the trenches.

Marines wave from "side-door Pullmans" on the way to a staging area.

nks onto rail cars. In all, 324 Allied tanks helped to break the German lines.

Despite a strong shove, an artillery horse balks at entering a freight car.

As the Yanks moved up, they found the Allies battered and weary from years of futile warfare. Here French poilus carry a corpse past a wounded comrade.

Amid the rubble of a shell-torn wood near Ypres, an Australian pauses to aid his fallen buddy. The conflict in this sector took nearly 250,000 lives in three months.

British infantry and tanks advance through a smoke screen during the August 1918 Amiens battle to achieve a historic victory of mechanized warfare.

At first the green Americans were assigned to quiet sectors, but by 1918 they were slugging away in such decisive battles as the Meuse-Argonne offensive, here being opened by a shelling from a 14-inch gun of the 35th Coast Artillery. Lacking the fatalistic caution of their battle-weary allies, the dough-boys charged into no man's land with a rash enthusiasm that turned out to be as effective militarily as it was costly for the first attack waves.

One American general noted proudly, "So insistent were the requests for American troops that it seemed that the commanders of our Allies felt that the very presence of American divisions assured victory." And the Germans were impressed too. Later, a German General Staff officer remarked, "The attack of the American troops, with the impetuosity which the German Staff had not believed possible, brought about the ruin of the German army."

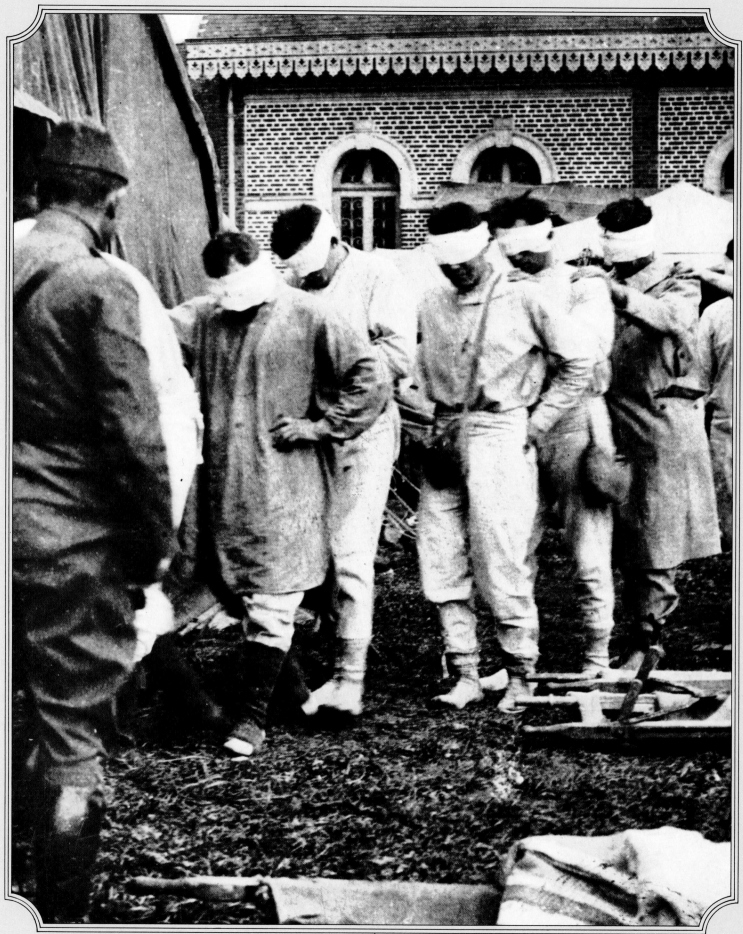

Doughboys blinded by gas line up at a field hospital before being sent to the rear for more treatment—which, unhappily, did not always restore their sight.

In a field near Saint-Mihiel, American soldiers pray at a comrade's funeral. By war's end, 50,300 Americans had been killed in action, 206,000 wounded.

An Album of Heroes

Correspondent Floyd Gibbons

First newspaper correspondent to be decorated for bravery under fire, Gibbons received the Croix de Guerre after being shot in the head and arm while going to the aid of a soldier in Belleau Wood.

Chaplain Francis Duffy

Though a man of the cloth, Father Duffy of the 69th Infantry proved so strong a leader under fire that his general, Douglas MacArthur, praised him as a potential commander of a field battalion.

Captain Eddie Rickenbacker

Captain Eddie—whose exploits in Paris were reputed to be equal to his conquests in the air—shot down 26 Boche planes in only seven months, setting the American record.

General John J. Pershing

America's greatest hero was "Black Jack" Pershing, Commander in Chief of the A.E.F. Strong-willed and 200 per cent American, he held U.S. troops together in a single effective army, refusing to parcel out his men to European commanders.

Sergeant Samuel Woodfill

Mild, modest Sergeant Woodfill performed one of the epic exploits of the war: alone, he knocked out five machine gun nests, then bashed in two Germans' heads with a pickax.

Sergeant Alvin York

To deeply religious Alvin York, the commandment "thou shalt not kill" was a divine law always to be obeyed. As a result, he originally sought draft exemption as a conscientious objector. Later, after he changed his mind, the Tennessee hillbilly became the most celebrated doughboy of all when he singlehandedly overpowered a German machine-gun battalion, taking 132 prisoners and leaving 25 dead.

Victory-flushed Yanks of the hard-hitting 16th Infantry, First Division, crowd around a piano left behind in Monsard, France, by hastily departing Germans

Tin-hatted and smiling, a squad of Salvation Army lasses welcomes hungry soldiers of the 26th Division with a table spread with fresh apple pies.

In a symbolic display of Allied solidarity, American soldiers, sailors and marines share sandwiches with a French officer at a Red Cross station in Bordeaux.

During one of the least beloved ceremonies of Army life, men of the 32nd Division strip to the buff near Montfaucon, France, to be sprayed for "cooties."

A Word from the Boys at the Front

For many Americans, the most treasured stories of the war came from the words of the boys at the front. These personal impressions carried home the terribly intimate feeling of battle often missing from the dispatches of professional reporters. The account of an aerial dogfight, told to fighter pilot and aviation chronicler Ted Parsons by his cohort Clyde Balsley of the Lafayette Escadrille—a squadron of U.S. pilots fighting under the French flag—carries an urgency that no earthbound newspaperman could have recorded. And the excerpts from soldiers' letters home reveal the gamut of feelings that confronted the men when they got down to the dirty business of killing.

It was dawn, a Sunday morning in June 1916. Four of us left our field at Bar-le-Duc to make our regular patrol. We made a long patrol from St. Mihiel to Verdun, getting well into the German lines in the early morning.

Across from Hill 305, while still back within the German territory, I saw a German plane. Further on, I saw more Germans. Then I began to watch my man. It looked like a good chance to pick him off. Diving steeply, I swung to the left to get in line. Down—down. I poised for decision. I would take him!

I held my fire—closer—closer. He was in my sights. I fired once —twice. These were my first and last shots. My machine gun had jammed! I pulled away, but a machine gun opened on my left, another on my right. I was surrounded. I swung in every direction, then through a cloud. Bullets followed. Black patches on my wing. I rolled over on my back. I was in another line of fire. The linen tore with the bursts. I was about twelve thousand feet up, and while I was on my back something struck me—like the kick of a mule. I had the sensation as though my leg were shot away and put my hand down to learn if it was still there.

My safety belt held or the blow would have knocked me overboard. I cut the motor. My legs were paralyzed. I fell into a tight spin. It was all over.

"Stop yourself." I was shouting it out loud. "Don't quit."

My mind cleared, and I tried to push my right leg into action. My feet, strapped to the rudder bar, straightened it up.

The spin was over. Where was I? My hand on my knee to keep the rudder straight, I leveled out. Crack—crack—crack.

Someone was still on my tail. My gun was still useless, both my legs were paralyzed. I could not maneuver, so down again I went, but this time under control. I looked at my altimeter. Only eight hundred meters up, but I kept on down to the treetops. I pulled out with an awful jerk. The wings stayed on. That last dive got me away. I put the switch on, my motor caught and I opened it up. It was my only hope. A long drive to the lines.

Hand on my knee to hold that rudder bar straight. Fifty feet over the trenches—then, no longer trenches but broken shell holes. Blue helmets—France!

I was bleeding badly and faint. Field of green—could I swing for it? I worked my rudder, turned and slid in for the field. Too late, I saw it was filled with barbed wire. I was landing between the front line and the reserve. I pancaked in.

Wheels in the wire, the Nieuport turned over and crashed. Gasoline was soaking me. I broke my belt and dropped out. Legs still paralyzed, afraid of fire, I tried to get to my knees. No hope. Caught onto the weeds, dragging myself along the ground like a dog with a broken back. A burst of dust in the field, no sound. My ears were gone from that terrific dive. The 77's dropped all around me. A direct hit on the ship. The shelling stopped. Four French soldiers crawled out of their trench, caught hold of me and dropped me down. I had made my last flight for France.

Dear Mother and All: *Somewhere in France*

I will tell you all the Huns are dirty people they will kill you anyway even drop booms on poor women and children while they are asleep. I am going to bring back that Germans teeth for you, don't be afraid I wont, that will be an easy thing to get. With love to all, Goodby.

Pvt. Curtis R. Hood

Dear Wife: *American Ex. Forces*

We pulled out about the 19th of Sept, moving towards the Argonne Forest. Finly we came to thair trenches and thair we got lots of prisiners, another fellow and myself got 13 out of one little dugout. We seen a machine gun setting in the mouth of the dugout so we stopped and decided what to do. So I asked him what he wanted to do, go get the machine gun or stay thair and keep his eye on the dugout until I could crawl up and get the gun, so he decided he would let me go.

Thair at that line of trenches one of the boys threw a hand grenade in on a Hun as he started to come out without his hands up and killed him. Well, it was along about eleven o'clock in the day now and as we hadnt had any breakfast we were getting quite tired and hungry.

In a short while we started to advance and by that time Jerry was sending shells over in a jiffy. Right thair was when I saw what war really was. The fellow on my right got hit. It was my luck that I was caught right in an open place so I dropped behind an old stump and thair I had to stay as it looked as if they were going to mow the old stump down. Well, I thought that I was a gone sucker sure. I laid thair until dark looking every minute for Fritzie to sneek up on me but he didn't come. Seven of us was sent back to gather up some ammunition and the Germans saw us and threw the shells into us. Three shells came all at once right on top of us. The man in front of me fell and the one in rear of me. The concussion from the explosion knocked me down and when I went to get up I was bured in dirt and rack and I thought I was killed as they almost knocked me senseless. Will leave out quite a bit that I witnessed now as it is too bad to write. We had 250 men when we started over the top on the 26th of Sept. and when we came out thair want but about 80 of us left. Gee, I did feel lucky, which all of us did that were still alive. Love to you.

Your Husband, Pvt. Jesse M. Maxey

To the editor of "The Sun":   *France, 1918*

The President says we are not fighting the Germans but Prussianism. But if he had seen what I have he would class all Huns as Huns and fight them tooth and nail. I was bloodthirsty. I bought a file to sharpen my bayonet to convince the Hun that there is a "war on." I was loaded down like a dromedary; I looked like a Christmas-tree all hung. Rifle, bayonet (keen-edged), grenades, a pick and shovel, umpty rounds ammunition, two packs of rations. All drest up and nowhere to go!

About four in the afternoon an officer came to me and said: "There's a Hun lying in the trench. Will you get him out?"

"Yes, I will get him out. I'll slit his throat."

I went up to the Hun—a big blue-eyed Saxon. He looked up at me and said: "Wilst du ich aus mocht?" ("Will you get me out?") One look at the poor devil and I drest his wounds and carried him the first lap on his journey to the hospital.

And thus died the last spark of frightfulness that was in me. I was not made of the same stuff the Hun was.

Hal B. Donnelly

Celebrating the long-awaited Armistice, servicemen and women joined the exuberant, flag-waving civilians parading down

Ziegfeld girls portray months of the year in the 1915 "Follies."

The Great White Way

The Broadway man has a better idea of life and things in general than any other class of man in the world. He sees more, meets more and absorbs more in a day than the average individual will in a month.

GEORGE M. COHAN

During the second decade Broadway was the entertainment capital of America, and possibly of the world. Every night three dozen marquees were ablaze with show titles, more than in London, far more than in Paris. Crowded between 34th and 50th Streets, Manhattan's theater district was synonymous with diamonds and pearls, conspicuous consumption and very late hours.

New York theater was also the taste maker of the nation. Although a few people were beginning to take movies seriously *(pages 50-83)*, it was the theater that produced the most fashionable dress styles, the latest dance steps, the snappiest jokes and slang. For America, New York was the center of everything modern, and in New York it was Broadway that both reflected and created fads.

The stylish showmen who dominated the theater district shrewdly recognized that the American public's taste ran to humor, sentimentality and spectacle, and their shows mirrored this taste. In 1916, for instance, of all the productions on Broadway only three were serious dramas. The rest were musicals, comedies, farces and revues. It was, in fact, during this decade that the revue came into its own. Such audience-wise producers as George M. Cohan and the Shubert brothers, Lee and J.J., were staging extravagant productions. The acknowledged master of the revue, however, was Florenz Ziegfeld, who served up a rich potpourri of America's most famous celebrities, funniest comedians and loveliest girls.

Revues were always on top of the news. Comedians parodied the popular comic strip characters Mutt and Jeff and a man in a pinafore gagged it up as Little Buttercup—a take-off on Mary Pickford. To give a show a little class, visiting Russian ballet dancers were featured, but the audience was just as happy to watch girls shuffling through the "Panama-Pacific Drag" in honor of the new Panama Canal.

Theatergoers were thrilled to feel that they were in on things, and they knew that they would be the first to hear Irving Berlin's latest hit and would see—and also soon be imitating—this season's new dance step. Women copied the gowns, mannerisms and hairdos of ballroom stylist Irene Castle. Men picked up racy patter from Eddie Cantor or homespun humor from Will Rogers. And, during this awkward period of transition from the innocent past into a more sophisticated future, Americans looked to the gaudy revues and glib comedies for hints about the "liberated" attitudes they were so desperate to achieve.

WEEK BEGINNING MONDAY EVENING, JUNE 12, 1916.
Matinees Wednesday and Saturday.

F. ZIEGFELD, Jr.

Offers

The 10th Anniversary Production of the

ZIEGFELD FOLLIES

Staged by Ned Wayburn

Book and Lyrics by George V. Hobart and Gene Buck.

Scenery by Joseph Urban

Music by Louis Hirsch, Jerome D. Kern and David Stamper.

ACT I.
PROLOGUE
THE BIRTH OF ELATION
Scene—In the Park of Phantasy
Characters

Puck	Miss Emma Haig
William Shakespeare	Mr. William Rock
George M. Cohan	Mr. Carl Randall
Follies Girl of 1907	Miss Gertrude Scott
Follies Girl of 1908	Miss Hazel Lewis
Follies Girl of 1909	Miss Gladys Loftus
Follies Girl of 1910	Miss Grace Jones
Follies Girl of 1911	Miss May Carmen
Follies Girl of 1912	Miss Tot Qualters
Follies Girl of 1913	Miss Helen Barnes
Follies Girl of 1914	Miss Gladys Feldman
Follies Girl of 1915	Miss Evelyn Conway
Follies Girl of 1916	Miss Allyn King

SCENE 2—THE STREET OF MASKS AND FACES
Characters

Mark Antony	Mr. Bernard Granville
A Roman Woman	Miss Ethel Callahan
A Man	Mr. Arthur Whitman
Julius Caesar	Mr. Don Barclay

SCENE 3—THE FORUM IN ROME
SONG—"Ragtime in the Air"..Julius Caesar and the Toga Girls

SCENE 4—IN THE GOLDEN CORRIDOR
Characters

William Shakespeare	Mr. William Rock
King Henry VIII	Mr. Sam B. Hardy
Ann Hathaway	Miss Frances White

SONG—"The Six Little Wives of the King"..Mr. Hardy and the Misses Davies, Conway, Lewis, Feldman, Tuey, Qualters
SONG—"I've Saved All My Lovin' For You"..Miss Frances White, Mr. Rock and Male Chorus

SCENE 5—TRAVESTY OF ROMEO AND JULIET
Scene—In the Backyard of the Capulets
Characters

Friar Lawrence	Mr. Clay Hill
Romeo	Mr. Bernard Granville
Juliet	Miss Ina Claire
Nurse	Miss Justine Johnstone

DUET—"Have a Heart"..Miss Claire and Mr. Granville

SCENE 6—ESCAPING THE MOVIES

Dance	Miss Ann Pennington

SONG—"Somnambulistic Melody"..Miss White and the Sparking Girls

SCENE 7—TRAVESTY OF OTHELLO
Scene—The Bedroom in Mr. and Mrs. Othello's Apartment
Characters

Emilia	Miss Helen Barnes
Iago	Mr. Sam B. Hardy
Othello	Mr. Bert Williams
Desdemona	Mr. Don Barclay

SCENE 8—SONG

"When the Lights Are Low"	Miss Claire

SCENE 9—ON THE BANKS OF THE NILE
Characters

Antony	Mr. Granville
Shakespeare	Mr. Rock
Cleopatra	Miss Allyn King

Ladies from Shakespeare's Plays:

Lady Macbeth	Miss Loftus
Viola	Miss Tashman
Mistress Page	Miss Feldman
Rosalind	Miss Conway
Ophelia	Miss Qualters
Desdemona	Miss Gunther
Juliet	Miss Davies
Miranda	Miss Paul
Katherine	Miss Hart
Portia	Miss Lewis

SONG—"Lady of the Nile"..Mr. Bernard Granville and Ensemble and Ensemble

SCENE 10—UNPREPAREDNESS
Scene—A Room in the Home of the Original Optimist
Characters

Uncle Sam	Mr. Sam B. Hardy
Columbia, his daughter	Miss Justine Johnstone
God of War	Mr. Peter Swift
Common People	Mr. Bernard Granville

DEFENCELESS AMERICA

Venus	Miss Allyn King

SCENE 11—SOMEWHERE IN THE NORTH SEA
(Illusion invented by Frank C. Thomas)
SCENE 12—RECRUITING ON BROADWAY
Characters

Spickan Spann, a recruiting officer	Mr. Sam B. Hardy
Hazza Gunn, a soldier	Mr. John Ryan
Suffern Smith	Mr. William Rock
Reddan Greene	Mr. William C. Fields
Baddan Tough	Mr. Peter Swift
Upall Day	Mr. Don Barclay
Maybee Knott	Mr. Bert Williams
Ima Cutey	Miss Helen Barnes

SCENE 13—IN FAR HAWAII
Characters

A Yankee Tourist	Mr. Bernard Granville
A Hula Dancer	Miss Ann Pennington
Ukalili Lou	Mr. Bert Williams
A Hawaiian Lady	Miss Ina Claire

Royal Hawaiian Players

FINALE—"I Left Her on the Beach at Honolulu"..Mr. Granville and Hawaiian Girls

ACT II.
SCENE 1—THE BLUSHING BALLET
The Ante-Room of the Harem

Dance	Miss Emma Haig and "Sylphides" Girls

A Suggestion of "La Spectre de la Rose" with Mr. Carl Randall as "Nijinski"

Travesty of Sheherazade
Characters

The Sultan	Mr. Sam B. Hardy
O. Shaw	Mr. William C. Fields
Zobeide	Mr. Don Barclay
Eunuch	Mr. Norman Blume
Nijinski	Mr. Bert Williams

SONG—"Nijinski"..Miss Fannie Brice and Male Chorus

SCENE 2—INTERLUDE
Mr. Rock and Miss White

DUET—"Ain't It Funny What a Difference Just Few Drinks Make?"
Miss Claire and Mr. Hardy

SCENE 3—IN A BACHELOR'S QUARTERS
SONG—"Good Bye Dear Old Bachelor Days"..Mr. Bernard Granville, Assisted by Miss Justine Johnstone and the Bachelor Girls

SCENE 4—PUCK'S PICTORIAL PALACE
Characters

Oberon	Miss Allyn King
Moonlight	Miss Helen Barnes
Peaseblossom	Miss Marion Davies
Moth	Miss Tot Qualters
Cobweb	Miss Gladys Feldman
Mustardseed	Miss Hazel Lewis
Josephus Daniels	Mr. William C. Fields
Jane Cowl	Miss Ina Claire
William Jennings Bryan	Mr. Don Barclay
Mary Pickford	Miss Ann Pennington
Lou-Tellegen	Mr. Sam B. Hardy
Geraldine Farrar	Miss Ina Claire
Theodore Roosevelt	Mr. William C. Fields
John D. Rockerfeller	Mr. William Rock
Theda Bara	Miss Fannie Brice
Villa	Mr. Bert Williams
Billie Burke	Miss Ina Claire

SONG—"I Want That Star"..Miss Ina Claire and Eight Little Billees

SCENE 5—A CROQUET GAME
On the Lawn at Lallypoosa
Characters

Mr. Zipp, a croquet player	Mr. William C. Fields
Mr. Zupp, a waiter	Mr. Sam B. Hardy

SCENE 6—FIFTH AVENUE
Characters

Stop-Go Girl	Miss Tot Qualters
Traffic Cop	Mr. Carl Randall
Miss Chief	Miss Marion Davies
Miss Understood	Miss Evelyn Conway
Miss Hap	Miss Hazel Lewis
Miss Behave	Miss May Carmen

SONG—"Stop and Go"..Mr. Randall and Avenue Girls

SONGS—MR. BERT WILLIAMS

Credits
Costumes designed by Cora McGeachy and Av O'Neil, and executed by Schneider-Anderson.
The siren gowns used in the Cleopatra barge scene are the creations of Lady Duff Gordon, also pink gowns.
Electric effects by Ben Beerwald.

The lavish program for the 1916 "Ziegfeld Follies" revue included a hula dancer, Shakespeare parodies, war skits and ballet—and the names of several theater greats.

Natty, poised and extravagant, Flo Ziegfeld traveled in private railroad cars, handed out bags of gold to friends and thought nothing of sending 14-page telegrams.

Glorifier of the American Girl

The United States' best-known connoisseur of female flesh was Florenz Ziegfeld. He made "Glorifying the American girl" his motto, and every year he interviewed some 15,000 applicants in order to skim off the cream for his spectacular *Follies*. Wearing spats and a pink shirt, the "Great Glorifier," as he was called, would sit in a darkened theater while an endless line of young hopefuls paraded past him on the stage. If a girl was called back, her heart—and mode of living—leaped: she had been elected to become a Ziegfeld Girl. Suddenly she was earning the extravagant salary of $75 a week and was on the threshold of a round of late-night suppers, dates with millionaires and frequent mentions in the gossip columns.

Ziegfeld's ideal requirements for a woman were: bust, 36; waist, 26; hips, 38. The emphasis was on the hips. Complexion didn't matter to him because he realized that beautiful skin and coloring do not show up on the stage. However, he did demand perfect teeth, lustrous hair and "personality." This last ingredient could come in either big packages or small. A typically large gem was the statuesque Dolores, whom Ziegfeld grabbed out of a fashion show and catapulted to stardom—with the exhortation that she just stand and look beautiful. The opposite type also appealed to Ziegfeld. One of his most sensational headliners was Marilyn Miller, only five feet three inches tall, but as Ziegfeld said, "the incarnation of freshness, of youth, of vitality." So famous did Ziegfeld become for his taste in women that he was asked to write for *American* magazine a detailed account of his specifications. He was the nation's arbiter of feminine beauty.

Once Ziegfeld had culled his jewels, he went to infinite lengths to display them properly. He had the girls drilled in their paces until split-second timing had become second nature. Sometimes his rehearsals lasted all night, and if a cast member was slow to learn, Ziegfeld could become, as one girl remarked, "Mr. Icewater." He spared no expense on costumes or sets. For one scene set in the Orient, Ziegfeld used 12 satin pillows that cost $300 apiece. Designer Joseph Urban created fantastic underwater effects for one scene, constructed gigantic fake elephants for another and propelled a swan boat across the stage in an "Antony and Cleopatra" episode.

Between the girlie numbers, Ziegfeld ran on a sequence of comics that amounted to a Who's Who of Broadway's laughgetters. Eddie Cantor might do a take-off called "The Osteopath." Fanny Brice would render "Rose of Washington Square" or lampoon the sultry Theda Bara. Will Rogers would drawl his way through rambling monologues on the current scene: "Congress is so strange. A man gets up to speak and says nothing. Nobody listens. Then everybody disagrees." Ziegfeld himself, however, was notably humorless and regarded his comedians as time-killers before Les Girls came on.

At the critical instant, the girls would enter to a lilting tune like Irving Berlin's "A Pretty Girl Is Like A Melody." Accenting the pelvis and lifting the shoulders, each girl

---

Ziegfeld took Michelangelo's statues, took some of the fat off them with a diet of lamb chops and pineapples, then he and Ben Ali Haggin brought the statues to life, only with better figures, and the only marble about them was from the ears north.

WILL ROGERS

---

would undulate slowly into the spotlight. She would be swathed in acres of feathers and chiffon (a single gown could cost $20,000). Aloof, expressionless, she would arrive at center stage, pause, then flash a quick smile before slinking slowly off. It never missed.

The languorous parades were all the more popular because the people out front had heard something about the madcap, scandal-ridden lives of these ravishing beauties, a few of whom are shown on the following pages. Everyone "knew," for example, that blonde Marion Davies was the girlfriend of the newspaper tycoon William Randolph Hearst, that Ann Pennington ran through a string of betrothals, that Olive Thomas was a nobody from the coal town of McKees Rocks, Pennsylvania, until she was discovered by Ziegfeld. In fact, scandalmongers reported that both Olive and Marilyn Miller were on intimate terms with none other than the Great Glorifier himself.

DOLORES --THE GIRL WHO NEVER SMILED

MARION DAVIES -- A FRIEND OF MR. HEARST

MARILYN MILLER--FLO'S FIVE-FOOT FAVORITE

OLIVE THOMAS -- DIAMOND FROM THE COAL COUNTRY

ANN PENNINGTON -- A MUCH ENGAGED BEAUTY

FANNY BRICE--VAMP FROM THE LOWER EAST SIDE

W.C. FIELDS

ED WYNN

NUT SUNDAY

ZIEGFELD'S COMEDIANS

*Although Ziegfeld lacked humor, he
had a fine eye for talent. He discovered
Will Rogers performing a rope-twirling
act. W. C. Fields was a juggler when
Ziegfeld hired him, and Leon Errol
had worked in burlesque. The comedians
pictured here convulsed "Follies"
audiences during the entire decade.*

BERT WILLIAMS

LEON ERROL

WILL ROGERS

Irving Berlin tinkles an upright piano in the only key he knew, F-sharp major. To change keys he had his piano rigged with a device that could transpose.

The King with One Key

Much of the music to which Ziegfeld's performers glided on stage—and to which the rest of America bounced or swayed on hometown dance floors—was the work of a five-foot-six-inch youth named Irving Berlin, a kid from New York's Lower East Side. When Berlin arrived on Broadway, at the age of 23, he had had two years of formal schooling, had never learned to read or write music, could play the piano only by ear and then only in one key.

Berlin's leap to fame came in 1911, on a song he tossed together in a hurry for a nonsense show. Invited to join the Friars Club, the show business fraternity, he was required as an initiate to come up with some sort of entertainment for the annual *Friars Frolics*. So he dug up a lyric he had written a year before, rewrote it to go with a new tune he dreamed up and presented it to the brothers. The tune was called "Alexander's Ragtime Band."

The Friars, who should have recognized a hit when they heard one, must have thought it was a bore. None of them rushed to publish or sing it, and the song went unnoticed until months later, when a songstress belted it out in a vaudeville show and brought the house down. A few months after that "Alexander's Ragtime Band" had sold a million copies of sheet music all across America; in a year it was the biggest ragtime hit of all time.

Other hits followed in quick succession, and Berlin's name was made. Soon he was writing songs for the celebrated Ziegfeld and other Broadway producers, and in between shows he turned out sheet after sheet of songs that were sung around parlor pianos. He was a versatile man who catered to every taste. His lyrics were comic, satiric or tender; his tunes were sometimes rag, sometimes gliding, always singable. The Berlin songs listed below, only a fraction of the 300 or so he turned out during the era, show something of his range. Mixed among the happy-go-lucky ragtime hits are sentimental ballads, war songs and even a jibe at Prohibition—"I'll See You in Cuba," a country where a thirsty man could still get a drink after January 1920. Together they echo the moods of the decade.

1910	1914	1917
CALL ME UP SOME RAINY AFTERNOON	HE'S A DEVIL IN HIS OWN HOME TOWN	DANCE AND GROW THIN
GRIZZLY BEAR	HE'S A RAG PICKER	IT TAKES AN IRISHMAN TO MAKE LOVE
	I WANT TO GO BACK TO MICHIGAN	WHOSE LITTLE HEART ARE YOU BREAKING NOW
1911	DOWN ON THE FARM	
ALEXANDER'S RAGTIME BAND	PLAY A SIMPLE MELODY	**1918**
EVERYBODY'S DOIN' IT NOW	THE SYNCOPATED WALK	DOWN WHERE THE JACK O'LANTERNS GROW
THE RAGTIME VIOLIN	WHEN IT'S NIGHT TIME IN DIXIE LAND	DREAM ON LITTLE SOLDIER BOY
THAT MYSTERIOUS RAG		I CAN ALWAYS FIND A LITTLE SUNSHINE
	1915	IN THE Y.M.C.A.
1912	ARABY	I'M GONNA PIN A MEDAL ON THE GIRL I LEFT BEHIND
RAGTIME SOLDIER MAN	THE GIRL ON THE MAGAZINE COVER	OH, HOW I HATE TO GET UP IN THE MORNING
WHEN I LOST YOU	I LOVE A PIANO	THEY WERE ALL OUT OF STEP BUT JIM
WHEN THE MIDNIGHT CHOO CHOO LEAVES	THAT HULA HULA	
FOR ALABAM'	WHEN I LEAVE THE WORLD BEHIND	**1919**
		MANDY
1913	**1916**	A PRETTY GIRL IS LIKE A MELODY
AT THE DEVIL'S BALL	EVERYTHING IN AMERICA IS RAGTIME	YOU CANNOT MAKE YOUR SHIMMY SHAKE ON TEA
SAN FRANCISCO BOUND	IN FLORIDA AMONG THE PALMS	
SNOOKEY OOKUMS	STOP, LOOK, LISTEN	**1920**
THAT INTERNATIONAL RAG	WHEN I'M OUT WITH YOU	I'LL SEE YOU IN CUBA
YOU'VE GOT YOUR MOTHER'S BIG BLUE EYES	WHEN THE BLACK SHEEP RETURNS TO THE FOLD	TELL ME LITTLE GYPSY

Wearing a boater and sporting a cane, George M. Cohan gives the lowdown to the boys in "The Little Millionaire," a musical farce that also starred Cohan's parents.

Mister Versatile

George M. Cohan was the most active figure in American theater during the decade. Only five feet six inches tall, he was a dynamo of energy. Belligerent, sentimental, a snappy dresser who jabbed everyone in the ribs and called him "Kid," Cohan was at once playwright, song writer, director, actor, dancer and producer. Working at top speed, he wrote his hit mystery, *Seven Keys to Baldpate*, in 10 days, operated his own theater on Times Square and was often involved with three or four productions at once. Below is a chart indicating the staggering range of his activities over the 10-year period.

MAJOR COHAN PRODUCTIONS

1910	GET-RICH-QUICK WALLINGFORD Wrote, produced, directed	comedy
1911	THE LITTLE MILLIONAIRE Wrote, produced, directed, acted in	musical farce
1912	FORTY-FIVE MINUTES FROM BROADWAY Wrote, produced, directed, acted in	musical comedy revival
1912	BROADWAY JONES Wrote, produced, directed, acted in	play
1913	SEVEN KEYS TO BALDPATE Wrote, produced, directed	mystery farce
1914	THE MIRACLE MAN Wrote, produced, directed	play
1914	HELLO BROADWAY Wrote, produced, directed, acted in	musical play
1915	HIT-THE-TRAIL HOLLIDAY Wrote, produced, directed	farce
1916	THE COHAN REVUE OF 1916 Wrote, produced, directed	revue
1917	OVER THERE Wrote	song
1918	THE COHAN REVUE OF 1918 Wrote, produced, directed	revue
1918	THREE FACES EAST Produced, directed	play
1918	A PRINCE THERE WAS Wrote, produced, directed	comedy
1918	THE VOICE OF McCONNELL Wrote, produced, directed	comedy
1919	THE ROYAL VAGABOND Produced, directed	opéra comique
1919	THE ACQUITTAL Produced	melodrama
1920	GENIUS AND THE CROWD Produced, directed	comedy
1920	THE MEANEST MAN IN THE WORLD Wrote, produced	comedy
1920	THE TAVERN Produced	melodrama

Darlings of the Dance Craze

Of all the stars that burst upon Broadway in the second decade, none had a greater impact on America than Vernon and Irene Castle, a pair of dancers who combined extraordinary grace and good looks. Their reign as the top personalities in show business was both brilliant and tragically brief. When they appeared on Broadway in 1914 in the musical *Watch Your Step*, America was in the throes of a dancing craze, bobbing and jiggling to a lively but ungraceful series of steps called the grizzly bear, the bunny hug and the turkey trot. Then the Castles glided into the limelight and their effortless style cried for imitation.

The Castles came upon their style almost by accident. As unemployed actors taking time off from Broadway slapstick for a honeymoon trip to Paris in 1912, Vernon and Irene got a job as a dance team at the sumptuous Café de Paris. The night before they were to go on, the Castles went to the café to see what the place was like. They got up from their table to dance, and because Irene was wearing her wedding dress as an evening gown, they had to tone down the high-stepping gymnastics that were the vogue. Their grace and ingenuity entranced the management, which asked them to dance just like that the following night. Soon the Castles had wowed all Paris.

Returning triumphantly to New York later in 1912, they set out on a dizzying round of Broadway musicals, cabaret engagements and ballroom exhibitions. Soon virtually everybody from debutantes to shopgirls had given up the turkey trot and other gyrations for the Castle Walk and the fox trot, two of Vernon's several inventions. In the rush to be just like the Castles, pillars of society such as John D. Rockefeller Jr. took tango lessons from Vernon at a fee of $100 an hour. And every woman in America secretly envied—or openly imitated—Irene's daring bobbed hair and her slim, uncorseted silhouette.

While the Castles led America to the peak of the dance craze, bluenoses disapproved. "I had seen drunken sailors cavorting in various ports in the world," croaked the writer William Inglis in *Harper's Weekly*, "but never anything like this in the presence of fathers, mothers and daughters." Most of America heartily disagreed. And even after the dashing Vernon was killed in a wartime plane crash, Americans continued to dance to the Castles' measure, as set down below in an excerpt from their book, *Modern Dancing*, and in articles like the one overleaf.

Modern dancing has come to stay, whatever may be the current opinion. Objections to dancing have been made on the ground that it is wrong, immoral and vulgar. This it certainly is not—when the dancers regard propriety. It is possible to make anything immoral and vulgar; all depends on how it is done.

A vulgar man or woman betrays lack of breeding even in walking across the room; sitting down may be performed in a vulgar manner, or any other smallest act. The modern dances properly danced are not vulgar in any way; on the contrary, they embody both grace and refinement; and impartial critics who have been called upon to pronounce judgment upon them have ended by saying that there is nothing at all objectionable in any of them.

They are, then, not immoral, not against any religious creed.

From the standpoint of health, dancing is fine exercise and keeps one absolutely fit. We ourselves can vouch for that, and we know of many people who looked 50 years of age three years ago and look less than 40 today. They owe it all to dancing. These facts are significant. Other facts are equally so. There was less champagne sold last year than in any one of the 10 previous years. People who dance drink less, and when they drink at all they exercise, instead of becoming torpid around a card table. There are so many arguments in favor of dancing that reasonable minds must be convinced that the present popularity of dancing is one of the best things that has happened in a long time.

Dancing gracefully in close embrace, Vernon and Irene Castle epitomize the easy-going mood that America sought as it rebelled against the stuffy strictures of the past.

ONE

We Commence by
Rocking Forward,
You on Your Right
and I on My Left
for Two Beats

TWO

Then We Rock
Back on the Other
Foot for Two Beats

THE CASTLE GAVOTTE

At the height of the dance craze, in 1914, Edward W. Bok, editor of the influential "Ladies' Home Journal," inaugurated a series of articles intended to show how dancing could be done with finesse—that is, in the fashion of Vernon and Irene Castle. The pictures on these pages, showing (counterclockwise) the Castle Gavotte as danced by its

THREE

In the Second Step
Your Part is Exactly
the Same: I Turn in
Front of You and Do
the Same Step Backward

FOUR

For the Next Step I am Still Facing
You, but My Position is at Your Side
Instead of Directly in Front

FIVE

We Can Turn
Independently of
Each Other and
Continue in the
Same Direction

TEN

Bowing at the End of the Dance is Not So Low and Sweeping as in the Olden Times

NINE

At the End of the Sixteenth Beat You Have Made the Complete Circle

inventors and explained in captions by Vernon, was the second in a projected series. "It was Mademoiselle Pavlowa who has shown how beautiful the Gavotte really is," said Mr. Castle in the accompanying text. But many of Bok's matronly readers raised such a moralistic hue and cry that the ordinarily doughty Bok dropped the series.

EIGHT

Showing the Position Taken While You Circle Around Me

SIX

Instead of Rocking Backward and Forward We Take Two Slow Steps Forward

SEVEN

I Remain in This Position While You Walk Completely Around Me

Taking their lead from Broadway's tastesetters, ballroom teachers from across the nation learn the latest jazz steps at the Dancing Masters' Convention, August 1917.

Picture Credits

Cover—Fabric design by John Martinez.

6 through 9—Bostwick-Frohardt Collection, owned by KMTV, Omaha. 10 through 13—Brown Brothers. 14,15—Collection of Tana Hoban and Edward Gallob. 16,17—Bostwick-Frohardt Collection, owned by KMTV, Omaha. 18,19—Culver Pictures. 20,21—Manchester Historic Association. 22—Front pages of the following newspapers—*The Atlanta Journal*, August 17, 1915; *The Boston Post*, April 22, 1910, and May 16, 1911; *Cleveland Plain Dealer*, August 5, 1914, courtesy Micro Photo Division: A Bell & Howell Company, Wooster, Ohio; *The Denver Post*, January 3, 1920, and January 16, 1920; *The Detroit Free Press*, July 28, 1919, courtesy Industrial Microfilm Company, Highland Park, Michigan; *San Francisco Examiner*, March 20, 1920, courtesy Micro Photo Division: A Bell & Howell Company, Wooster, Ohio; the New York *World*, March 26, 1911, courtesy the New York Public Library. 25—Headlines from the front page of the Pittsburgh *Gazette Times*, November 8, 9, 10, 1916. 26,27—"A Tale of Today," from *Harper's Weekly*, February 13, 1915, pp. 160-161, reprinted by permission of Harper & Row, Publishers. 28,29—New York State Historical Association, Cooperstown. 31—United Press International. 32—Culver Pictures—Brown Brothers. 33—Title Insurance and Trust Co. (Los Angeles), collection of Historical Photographs—United Press International. 34,35—Minnesota Historical Society; Harris & Ewing from Gilloon Agency; Courtesy B. Altman & Co. 36,37—Courtesy The Public Library of Newark, from *The Delineator*, 1910 (Paulus Leeser); Sy Seidman, from *The Delineator*, 1914 (Paulus Leeser); from *The Delineator*, 1917 (Paulus Leeser); from *The Delineator*, 1920 (Paulus Leeser). 38,39—Armin F. Schmidt. 40—From *Life*, 1915—from *Life*, 1918—from *Life*, 1912. 42,43—The Missouri Historical Society. 44,45—Top, United Press International; Library of Congress; Culver Pictures, bottom, Library of Congress; Underwood and Underwood. 47—Schlesinger Library, Radcliffe College. 48,49—The Bettmann Archive. 50,51—Brown Brothers. 53—Historical Collections, Security Pacific National Bank, Los Angeles. 54—The Museum of Modern Art, Film Stills Archive. 57—Culver Pictures. 60,61—Culver Pictures. 62—The Bettmann Archive; The Academy of Motion Picture Arts and Sciences—Culver Pictures; The Museum of Modern Art, Film Stills Archive. 63—Culver Pictures. 64,65—R.R. Stuart Collection, Hollywood. 66—Sy Seidman. 68—Paramount Pictures; Culver Pictures. 69—Culver Pictures. 70—University of Texas; from *Pearl White the Peerless, Fearless Girl* by Raymond Lee and Manuel Weltman, A.S. Barnes & Co., Inc. 71—Culver Pictures. 72,73—Culver Pictures; The Museum of Modern Art, Film Stills Archive. 74—The Museum of Modern Art, Film Stills Archive except top left The Bettmann Archive. 75—Collection of Kevin Brownlow; Culver Pictures—The Academy of Motion Picture Arts and Sciences; The Museum of Modern Art, Film Stills Archive. 77,78,79—The Museum of Modern Art, Film Stills Archive. 80—The Academy of Motion Picture Arts and Sciences—Culver Pictures. 81—Collection of Kevin Brownlow—Culver Pictures. 82,83—The Academy of Motion Picture Arts and Sciences. 84,85—Culver Pictures. 87—Courtesy of the Henry Ford Museum, Dearborn, Michigan (Bradley Smith). 88,89—Courtesy of the Ford Archives, Henry Ford Museum, Dearborn, Michigan. 90—Automotive History Collection, Detroit Public Library—Culver Pictures. 91—Automotive History Collection, Detroit Public Library. 92—Library of Congress. 93—Culver Pictures. 94,95—Courtesy of the Ford Archives, Henry Ford Museum, Dearborn, Michigan. 96,97—Brown Brothers. 99,101,102—Courtesy of the Ford Archives, Henry Ford Museum, Dearborn, Michigan. 104,105—The National Archives. 106,107—Culver Pictures. 109—*Collier's*, September 30, 1911, courtesy A. William Barney (William Abbenseth). 110—*Life*, April 13, 1911 (Peter Christopoulous); *Good Housekeeping*, December 1916, reprinted by permission of *Good Housekeeping* magazine, © 1916 by the Hearst Corporation (Paulus Leeser)—*Good Housekeeping*, April 1919, reprinted by permission of *Good Housekeeping* magazine, © 1919 by the Hearst Corporation (Paulus Leeser); *Vogue*, June 15, 1917, courtesy of *Vogue*, copyright © 1917, 1945 by The Condé Nast Publications Inc. (from Culver Pictures). 111—*Ladies' Home Journal*, February 1913, courtesy of The Curtis Publishing Co. (Paulus Leeser). 112—*The Saturday Evening Post*, May 20, 1916, courtesy of The Curtis Publishing Co. (Paulus Leeser). 114—Arthur William Brown frontispiece

from *Seventeen* by Booth Tarkington, copyright, 1915, 1916 by the Metropolitan Magazine Company, reprinted by permission of Harper & Row, Publishers. 115—Montgomery Ward & Co. Catalogue Nos. 85 (1916-1917), 87 (1917), 92 (1920), and 93 (1920). 116—Brown Brothers; courtesy Max Eastman; Library of Congress. 117—Brown Brothers except center Keystone View Co., Inc. 118 through 125—From *The Masses*, courtesy Dr. Joseph Locke Slater, Colgate University, Hamilton, New York, except page 120 reprinted by permission of Quadrangle Books, Inc., from *Echoes of Revolt: The Masses, 1911-1917*, edited by William L. O'Neill, copyright © 1966 by Quadrangle Books, Inc. 127—The Gene Lovitz Memorial, Carl Sandburg Collection, Knox College, Galesburg, Illinois; Brown Brothers. 128—Courtesy Mrs. William Carlos Williams; Brown Brothers. 129—Keystone View Co., Inc.; courtesy Elenor Ruggles. 130,131—The University of Iowa Libraries, Iowa City; The Redpath Bureau, Chicago. 132 through 139—The Redpath Bureau, Chicago except page 137, far left, Hawaiian from Bourquin Collection, Kenneth Spencer Research Library, University of Kansas, Lawrence. 140,141—New York State Historical Association, Cooperstown. 143—Bostwick-Frohardt Collection, owned by KMTV, Omaha. 144—David R. Phillips, Chicago. 145—Collection of Tana Hoban and Edward Gallob. 146—Ellison Photo Company, Austin, Texas. 147—Library of Congress. 148,149—New York State Historical Association, Cooperstown. 150—Bostwick-Frohardt Collection, owned by KMTV, Omaha. 151—Library of Congress. 152, 153—New York State Historical Association, Cooperstown. 154,155—Sy Seidman. 157—Gene Laurents (courtesy Jerry Smith Collection and The Hallmark Gallery). 158,159—Car and plane from Montgomery Ward & Co. Catalogue and Buyers' Guide No. 93 (1920)—milk wagon and bicycle from Culver Pictures; Gene Laurents (courtesy Jerry Smith Collection and The Hallmark Gallery). 160,161—Gene Laurents (courtesy Jerry Smith Collection and The Hallmark Gallery, posters from Sy Seidman); Louis H. Hertz, *Handbook of Old American Toys*, Mark Haber & Co., Wethersfield, Connecticut, 1947, p. 96. 162, 163—Montgomery Ward & Co. Catalogue No. 93 (1920); Gene Laurents (courtesy Jerry Smith Collection and The Hallmark Gallery). 164—University of Washington. 166,167—David R. Phillips, Chicago. 168,169—New York State Historical Association, Cooperstown. 170,171—Brown Brothers. 172 through 177—*Oh Skinnay! The Days of Real Sport* by Briggs. Verses by Wilbur D. Nesbit. Published by P.F. Volland & Co., Chicago, 1913. Courtesy of the State Historical Society of Wisconsin. 178,179—Minnesota Historical Society (J.W.G. Dunn Collection). 180 through 191—Otto M. Jones Collection, Library of Congress. 192,193,195,202,203—Minnesota Historical Society. 196,197,199,200,201,204,205—*St. Paul Dispatch*. 198—St. Paul Winter Carnival Association. 206,207—The National Archives. 209—Minnesota Historical Society. 210,211—Culver Pictures; courtesy Huntington Hartford, New York. 212—The National Archives. 213—Michigan Historical Commission, Lansing. 214,215—The National Archives; Warshaw Collection of Business Americana. 216—The National Archives. 217—The Bettmann Archive. 218, 219—The National Archives; courtesy Huntington Hartford, New York. 220,221—The National Archives. 222,223—Courtesy Huntington Hartford, New York; The National Archives. 224,225—Young Men's Christian Association (Herbert Orth); Brown Brothers. 226,227—The National Archives; The National Archives—Brown Brothers. 228,229—Courtesy Huntington Hartford, New York; Culver Pictures. 230,231—The National Archives. 232,233—New York State Historical Association, Cooperstown. 234—Culver Pictures. 236—Minnesota Historical Society. 239—State Historical Society of Wisconsin. 241—The National Archives. 242,243—The National Archives except top left Culver Pictures, top center U.S. Air Force. 244—Musée des Armées, Vincennes. 245—Imperial War Museum, London—Imperial War Museum, London, courtesy American Heritage. 246 through 249—The National Archives. 250—Culver Pictures; courtesy United Artists Television—The Bettmann Archive; Culver Pictures; Wide World, courtesy *The New York Times*. 251—Brown Brothers. 252—The National Archives. 253—University of California, Los Angeles, Powell Library—The National Archives. 256,257—*The New York Times*. 258 through 261—Culver Pictures. 262—The Bettmann Archive. 264 through 269—Culver Pictures. 270,271—Culver Pictures except far right Brown Brothers. 272—Brown Brothers. 274,275—Culver Pictures. 277—Brown Brothers. 278,279—From *Ladies' Home Journal*, November 1914, © The Curtis Publishing Co. 280, 281—United Press International.

Acknowledgments

The editors of this book wish to thank the following persons and institutions for their assistance:

Academy of Motion Picture Arts and Sciences, Hollywood; Carl Backman, Manager, Western Division, Redpath Bureau, Chicago; Thomas Barrow, Assistant Curator of the Research Center, George Eastman House, Rochester, New York; Amelia D. Bielaski, Curator, Smith-Telfer Collection, New York State Historical Association, Cooperstown; James J. Bradley, Automotive History Collection, Detroit Public Library; Russell Chalberg, Ellison Photo Company, Austin; The Chicago Public Library; Harry Collins, Brown Brothers; Margaret Copeland, Historian, and Maritza Morgan, Chautauqua Institution, Chautauqua, New York; John Cumming, Director of Clarke Historical Library, Central Michigan University, Mt. Pleasant, Michigan; Virginia Daiker, Prints and Photographs Division, Library of Congress; John B. Danby, Executive Editor, Evangeline Pettrakis, Administrative Assistant, and Vivian Wilkinson, *Good Housekeeping;* Camille Duane, Institute of Texan Cultures, San Antonio; Max Eastman, New York City; Mrs. Ruth K. Field, Curator of Pictures, Missouri Historical Society, St. Louis; Dorothy Gimmestad, Assistant Picture Curator, Minnesota Historical Society, St. Paul; The Hallmark Gallery, New York City; Burnet Hershey, New York City; Dale Hoaglan, KMTV, Omaha; Charles Irby, Curator, Gernsheim Collection, University of Texas, Austin; Jack Krueger, Executive Editor, *Dallas Morning News;* Labor History Archives of Wayne State University, Detroit; Robert D. Monroe,

Chief of Special Collections, University of Washington, Seattle; Josephine Motylewski, The National Archives, Washington, D.C.; Sol Novin, Culver Pictures, New York City; Mrs. Jenny Padinger, Librarian, The Curtis Publishing Company, New York City; Frank Paluka, Special Collections, University of Iowa Libraries, Iowa City; Victor R. Plukas, Security Pacific National Bank, Los Angeles; Captain Kenneth H. Powers, 69th Regiment Armory, New York City; George Pratt, Associate Curator of Motion Pictures, George Eastman House, Rochester, New York; Mrs. Elizabeth Rademacher, Michigan Historical Commission Archives, Lansing; Paul Redding, Buffalo and Erie County Historical Society, Buffalo; Mrs. Jane E. Riss, Curator, Regional History Division, University of Kansas Libraries, Lawrence; Winthrop Sears Jr., Henry Ford Museum, Dearborn, Michigan; Sy Seidman, New York City; Mrs. Margaret Shepherd, Utah Historical Society, Salt Lake City; Jerry Smith, Kansas City, Missouri; Mrs. Bertha Stratford, Librarian, Museum of History and Industry, Seattle; Minor Wine Thomas Jr., Assistant Director, New York State Historical Association, Cooperstown; Mrs. Judith Topaz, Assistant, Iconographic Collections, State Historical Society of Wisconsin, Madison; Howard Willoughby, San Francisco; Mrs. Geneva Kebler Wiskemann, Reference Archivist, Michigan Historical Commission Archives, Lansing; Mary Yushak, Museum of Modern Art, New York City.

Bibliography

Baral, Robert, *Revue, A Nostalgic Reprise of the Great Broadway Period.* Fleet Publishing Corp., 1962.

Brown, Milton W., *The Story of the Armory Show.* The Joseph H. Hirshhorn Foundation, 1963.

Case, Victoria, and Robert Ormond Case, *We Called It Culture.* Doubleday & Co., 1948.

Castle, Irene, *Castles in the Air.* Doubleday & Co., 1958.

Churchill, Allen, *The Improper Bohemians.* E. P. Dutton & Co., 1959.

Churchill, Allen, *Over Here!* Dodd, Mead & Co., 1968.

Clymer, Floyd, *Henry's Wonderful Model T, 1908-1927.* McGraw-Hill Book Company, 1955.

Farnsworth, Marjorie, *The Ziegfeld Follies.* G. P. Putnam's Sons, 1956.

Higham, John, *Strangers in the Land.* Rutgers University Press, 1963.

Kramer, Dale, *Chicago Renaissance.* Appleton-Century, 1966.

Lahue, Kalton C., and Terry Brewer, *Kops and Custards: The Legend of Keystone Films.* University of Oklahoma Press, 1967.

Lord, Walter, *The Good Years.* Harper & Row, 1960.

McClintock, Inez and Marshall, *Toys in America.* Public Affairs Press, 1961.

MacLaren, Gay, *Morally We Roll Along.* Little, Brown & Co., 1938.

Mantle, Burns, and Garrison P. Sherwood, eds., *The Best Plays of 1909-1919.* Dodd, Mead & Co., 1945.

Mason, Herbert M. Jr., *The Lafayette Escadrille.* Random House, 1964.

May, Henry F., *The End of American Innocence.* Alfred A. Knopf, 1959.

Mock, James R., and Cedric Larson, *Words That Won the War.* Princeton University Press, 1939.

Morehouse, Ward, *George M. Cohan, Prince of the American Theater.* J. B. Lippincott Co., 1943.

National American Woman Suffrage Association, *Victory, How Women Won It.* H. W. Wilson Co., 1940.

Nevins, Allan, *Ford: The Times, the Man, the Company.* Charles Scribner's Sons, 1954.

O'Neill, William L., ed., *Echoes of Revolt: The Masses, 1911-1917.* Quadrangle Books, 1966.

Preston, William, Jr., *Aliens and Dissenters.* Harvard University Press, 1963.

Ramsaye, Terry, *A Million and One Nights: A History of the Motion Picture.* Simon & Schuster, 1926.

Renshaw, Patrick, *The Wobblies.* Doubleday Co., 1967.

Slosson, Preston W., *The Great Crusade and After: 1914-1928.* The Macmillan Co., 1930.

Stern, Philip Van Doren, *Tin Lizzie.* Simon & Schuster, 1955.

Sullivan, Mark, *Our Times.* Vols. 4-5. Charles Scribner's Sons, 1932, 1933.

Taft, Philip, *Organized Labor in American History.* Harper & Row, 1964.

Valentine, Alan, *1913: America Between Two Worlds.* The Macmillan Company, 1962.

Text Credits

113—"Speaking of Operations" by Irvin S. Cobb, *The Saturday Evening Post,* November 6, 1915. 114,115—From *Seventeen* by Booth Tarkington, pp. 104-108. Copyright, 1915, 1916 by the Metropolitan Magazine Company; renewed 1943, 1944 by Booth Tarkington. Reprinted by permission of Harper & Row, Publishers, and courtesy Booth Tarkington's heirs. 127—From "After Apple-Picking" from *Complete Poems of Robert Frost.* Copyright 1930, 1939 by Holt, Rinehart and Winston, Inc. Copyright © 1958 by Robert Frost. Copyright © 1967 by Lesley Frost Ballantine. Reprinted by permission of Holt, Rinehart and Winston, Inc.—from "Chicago" from *Chicago Poems* by Carl Sandburg. Copyright 1916 by Holt, Rinehart and Winston, Inc. Copyright 1944 by Carl Sandburg. Reprinted by permission of Holt, Rinehart and Winston, Inc.—From "The Young Housewife" from William Carlos Williams' *Collected Earlier Poems,* copyright 1938 by William Carlos Williams. Reprinted by permission of New Directions Publishing Corp.—from "Lilacs" from *Complete Poetical Works of Amy Lowell.* Reprinted by permission of

Houghton Mifflin. 129—From "The Congo" from *In the Congo and Other Poems* by Vachel Lindsay. Copyright 1914. Reprinted by permission of The Macmillan Company—from "The Hill" from *Spoon River Anthology* by Edgar Lee Masters. Copyright by The Macmillan Company, 1914, 1915, 1942. Reprinted by permission of Ellen C. Masters. 171—From *Penrod* by Booth Tarkington. Copyright 1914 by Doubleday & Company, Inc. Reprinted by permission of Doubleday & Company, Inc., and courtesy Booth Tarkington's heirs. 208—"Long Boy" by William Herschell and Barclay Walker. Copyright 1927, Shapiro, Bernstein & Co., Inc., New York. Copyright renewed. Used by permission. 212,213—"Dere Mable" by Edward Streeter. Copyright 1945, Edward Streeter. Used by permission. 254—Courtesy the estate of Rear Admiral Edwin C. Parsons. 255—Letters of Private Hood, Private Maxey from *Our Soldiers Speak, 1775-1918* by William Matthews and Dixon Wecter, Little, Brown and Company, 1943, pp.336-337, 311-321. 276—From *Modern Dancing* by Mr. & Mrs. Vernon Castle. Copyright 1914, renewed © 1941, pp. 31-33.

Index

Numerals in italics indicate an illustration of the subject mentioned.